PREDICTING PRESIDENTIAL ELECTIONS
AND OTHER THINGS, SECOND EDITION

PREDICTING PRESIDENTIAL

ELECTIONS AND OTHER THINGS,

SECOND EDITION

Ray C. Fair

Stanford Economics and Finance
An Imprint of Stanford University Press
Stanford, California

Stanford University Press
Stanford, California

Special discounts for bulk quantities of Stanford Economics and Finance are available to corporations, professional associations, and other organizations. For details and discount information, contact the special sales department of Stanford University Press. Tel: (650) 736-1782, Fax: (650) 736-1784

Printed in the United States of America on acid-free, archival-quality paper

Library of Congress Cataloging-in-Publication Data
Fair, Ray C., author.
   Predicting presidential elections and other things / Ray C. Fair.—
Second edition.
      pages cm
   Includes bibliographical references and index.
   ISBN 978-0-8047-6049-2 (cloth : alk. paper)
   1. Social prediction.   2. Presidents—United States—Elections—Forecasting.
3. Election forecasting—United States.   4. Economic forecasting.   I. Title.
HM901.F35 2011
303.4973—dc22

2011015106

Typeset by Newgen in 10/13.5 Sabon

тм
901
F35
2012
Contents

Preface

Since the first edition of this book was published in 2002, there have been two presidential elections, and I have added congressional elections to the analysis of voting behavior. This edition incorporates the new data and analysis. Two other studies have also been added, one on baseball and one on football. The original aim of this book remains the same—to present in an intuitive and nontechnical way tools and methods of the social sciences. The examples have been chosen to appeal to a broad range of interests—politics, sex, wine, grades, running, baseball, football, interest rates, and inflation. The first edition of this book has been used as a supplement to some introductory social science courses, especially introductory econometrics courses, and this edition should continue to serve this purpose.

Much of the data used in this book are available on my Web site: fairmodel.econ.yale.edu. Many of the results in this book can be reproduced using these data. Also, the Web site contains updated predictions of the presidential and congressional elections as new economic data become available.

My wife, Sharon Oster, and my children, Emily Fair Oster, Stephen Oster Fair, and John Fair Oster, were a great inspiration and help to me on the first edition, and they continue to keep me in check. John is the coauthor on the football analysis. Others who have provided useful comments include Orley Ashenfelter, John Covell, Fred Djang, John Ferejohn, Andrew Leigh, Jennifer Nou, and Terry Seaks. Soon after the first edition was published, Ken MacLeod, my editor and the one truly responsible for seeing the book through to completion, passed away. He is greatly missed. Margo Crouppen has been the energy and force behind this edition; I am indebted to her tireless efforts.

Ray Fair
New Haven, November 2010

PREDICTING PRESIDENTIAL ELECTIONS AND OTHER THINGS, SECOND EDITION

Introduction   **What This Book Is About**

If you have glanced at the Contents, you might be wondering what the topics in this book could possibly have in common. They include presidential and congressional elections, extramarital affairs, wine quality, college grades, marathon times, baseball performance, college football games, interest rates, and inflation. The answer is that they can all be explained and analyzed using the tools of the social sciences and statistics. The aim of this book is to allow those who are not necessarily well versed in these tools to see how this is done. The widely differing topics have been chosen to show the broad range of these tools and their strengths and weaknesses.

This book does not require that you be social scientists or statisticians or even that you like them. It is also fine if you don't know a Greek letter from a happy face emoticon. The book simply requires some patience in following the movement from a general idea of how something works to a specific prediction of what it will be in the future. The steps involved in this process can be explained without resort to technical material. By the end of the book, you should have a deeper understanding not only of the particular topics discussed but also of the way topics like these can be analyzed.

Knowledge of social science procedures allows a more critical reading of opinions and predictions that we are bombarded with every day. Is there any support for the particular opinion? How might the opinion be tested? How much confidence can be placed in the prediction? The problem of evaluating views is harder than ever now that we are in the Internet age. Information is available at the click of a mouse, and views can be backed up by vast amounts of information. But is the information any good?

Consider, for example, the topic of U.S. presidential elections. What factors are important in deciding who will win an election? There are many views. Some stress the personalities of the candidates, others stress the amount of money available to the campaigns, still others stress the economy, and so on. Although each view has a story with it, the problem is that there are too many stories. How do we separate the wheat from the chaff? We need some way of deciding which stories have something to them and which do not. One way comprises tools of the social sciences and statistics, which this book discusses. We will see that past election results can be used in a systematic way to decide which stories appear to have merit. But we can do more than this. We can also use the information from past elections to *predict* the outcome of an election that has not yet taken place. We can both explain, in terms of telling a story that seems consistent with past results, and predict.

So, what are these mysterious tools? We begin with some question of interest, such as what determines the outcomes of presidential elections? Why did Richard Nixon beat George McGovern in 1972, and why did Ronald Reagan beat Jimmy Carter in 1980? We usually have some initial ideas about the answer to our question. The economy may play an important role in influencing how people vote, so an obvious preliminary idea is that the economy affects voting behavior. Another obvious initial idea is that an incumbent president running again may have an advantage because he can use the powers of the presidency to try to sway voters.

We call an idea or a set of ideas offered to explain something a *theory*. A theory may or may not be a good explanation. For example, a theory that says that people vote for a candidate solely on the basis of his or her height is not likely to be a good explanation of the way people actually vote. A theory need not be original with you, and it does not really matter where it came from. What is important is that there is some way to test whether the theory is any good.

How would one test the theory that the economy affects voting behavior? This is where past election results come into play. We can collect data on the economy and on past election outcomes and see how closely the theory explains the data. Was it generally the case that the incumbent party won when the economy was good and lost when the economy was bad? This movement from proposing a theory to testing the theory using data is what most of this book is about. We will see that an important feature about testing theories is that once the tests have been performed, it is usually possible to move fairly easily to prediction.

The topics in this book have been chosen to appeal to a wide range of people. Political junkies and others interested in voting behavior should find the results on presidential and congressional elections helpful in understanding how people vote. Other dimensions of human behavior are covered in the chapters on extramarital affairs and college grades. In the chapter on extramarital affairs, we examine the factors that increase or decrease the chances that someone will have an affair. In the chapter on college grades, we examine how class attendance affects grades. As those of us who teach college students know, not every student shows up for every class. Does this matter in terms of grades and, if so, how much?

The chapter on wine quality shows that the quality a new wine eventually achieves after proper aging can be predicted fairly well simply by knowing the weather in the harvest year. This knowledge can help one decide whether a new wine is under- or overpriced and thus whether one should purchase it.

More serious investment issues are the concern of the chapters on interest rates and inflation. These chapters discuss how interest rates and inflation can be explained and predicted. This is the macroeconomic part of the book.

The chapter on marathon times should be of special interest to people older than age 35. It gives estimates of how fast people slow down as they age. If you are a runner older than 35 and have noticed that you are not quite as fast as you used to be, you can see if you are slowing down faster than you should be. The nice thing about this chapter is that it shows you need not feel bad just because you are slowing down. You only need to feel bad if you are slowing down too fast!

There are also chapters on baseball and football. The aim in the baseball chapter is to estimate aging effects. At what age do players peak, how fast do they improve up to the peak age, and how fast do they decline after the peak age? We will see that once we have estimated these effects, we have a better measure than simple lifetime averages to rank players. We can also use the results to examine unusual, possibly drug-aided, performances at the older ages.

The aim in the football chapter is to see if there is independent information in the various college football computer rankings in predicting point spreads. Can we combine the various computer rankings to produce a better ranking than any one individual ranking? The answer is yes. We will see, however, that the Las Vegas betting spread completely dominates all the rankings, even the best combination. All useful information is in the betting spread. The betting markets are efficient in this sense.

This book may also appeal to college students taking introductory courses in the social sciences and statistics. It provides an intuitive discussion of the tools used in these courses and contains a number of examples of their use. It is often said that the three main interests of college students are sex, drinking, and sports, with perhaps grades ranked fourth. This book has all four!

The most difficult chapter in the book is Chapter 2, which discusses the tools. The chapter is divided into seven lessons, one for each day of the week. Lesson 4 on Thursday is the hardest. It explains a key test statistic, the *t-statistic*, showing why a *t*-statistic greater than about 2 is supportive of the theory being tested, whereas smaller values are not. If you are willing to accept this result—that large *t*-statistics support a theory but small ones do not—on faith, you can skip Lesson 4. You will miss an explanation of why this is true, but it should not hinder your reading the rest of the book. Also, if the material in Chapter 2 is completely new to you, you may want to read the chapter quickly the first time through and then come back to it as you go through the examples in Chapters 3 and beyond.

The tools in Chapter 2 are best explained with an example, and we use voting behavior in presidential elections as the example. Chapter 1 introduces this topic. It presents a theory of what determines votes for president and discusses the data that are available to test the theory. This sets the stage for Chapter 2, which explains the tools. Chapter 3 continues the discussion of presidential elections using the tools from Chapter 2. Each of the remaining chapters is a separate topic, each using the tools from Chapter 2. These chapters need not be read in order, although Chapter 11 on interest rates should be read before Chapter 12 on inflation. There is a glossary at the end of the book of key words and concepts. The Chapter Notes at the end of the book give references.

In his advice to Harvard students in *Under Which Lyre*, W. H. Auden wrote:

> Thou shalt not answer questionnaires
> Or quizzes upon World-Affairs,
>   Nor with compliance
> Take any test. Thou shalt not sit
> With statisticians nor commit
>   A social science.

Alas, I am giving the opposite advice. Come sit with statisticians and social scientists for a while and see what they can do.

1   It's the Economy, Stupid

Election night at midnight:
Boy Bryan's defeat.
Defeat of western silver.
Defeat of the wheat.
Victory of letterfiles
And plutocrats in miles
With dollar signs upon their coats,
Diamond watchchains on their vests and spats on their feet.

Vachel Lindsay, from Bryan, Bryan, Bryan, Bryan

A common pastime in the United States every four years is predicting presidential elections. Polls are taken almost daily in the year of an election, and there are Web sites that allow betting on elections.

Some of the more interesting footnotes to presidential elections concern large errors that were made in predicting who would win. In 1936, the *Literary Digest* predicted a victory for Republican Alfred Landon over Democrat Franklin Roosevelt by a fairly large margin, when in fact Roosevelt won election to a second term by a landslide. The *Literary Digest* polled more than 2 million people, so the sample size was huge, but the sample was selected from telephone directories and automobile registrations, which overrepresented wealthy and urban voters, more of whom supported Landon. In addition, the response rate was higher for voters who supported Landon. The *Literary Digest* never really recovered from this error, and it ceased publication in 1938.

Another famous error was made by the *Chicago Tribune* in 1948, when it ran the headline "Dewey Wins." After it became clear that Thomas Dewey had lost, a smiling Harry Truman was photographed holding up the headline.

A more recent large error was made in June 1988, when most polls were predicting Michael Dukakis beating George Bush by about

17 percentage points. A few weeks later, the polls began predicting a Bush victory, which turned out to be correct.

While interesting in their own right, polls are limited in helping us understand what motivates people to vote the way they do. Most polls simply ask people their voting plans, not how or why they arrived at these plans. We must go beyond simple polling results to learn about the factors that influence voting behavior. This is where tools of the social sciences and statistics can be of help.

A Theory of Voting Behavior

To examine the question of why people vote the way they do, we begin with a theory. Consider a person entering a voting booth and deciding which lever to pull for president. Some people are dyed-in-the-wool Republicans and always vote for the Republican candidate. Conversely, others are dyed-in-the-wool Democrats and always vote Democratic. For some, one issue, such as abortion or gun control, dominates all others, and they always vote for the candidate on their side of the issue. For these people, there is not much to explain. One could try to explain why someone became a staunch Republican or Democrat or focused on only one issue, but this is not the main concern here. Of concern here are all the other voters, whom we will call *swing voters*. Swing voters are those without strong ideological ties and whose views about which party to vote for may change from election to election. For example, Missouri is considered a swing state (that is, a state with many swing voters). It sometimes votes Democratic and sometimes Republican. Massachusetts, on the other hand, almost always votes Democratic, regardless of the state of the economy or anything else, and Idaho almost always votes Republican. The percentage of swing voters in these two states is much smaller than the percentage in Missouri.

What do swing voters think about when they enter the booth? One theory is that swing voters think about how well off financially they expect to be in the future under each candidate and vote for the candidate under whom they expect to be better off. If they expect that their financial situation will be better off under the Democratic candidate, they vote for him or her; otherwise, they vote for the Republican candidate. This is the theory that people "vote their pocketbooks." The theory need not pertain to all voters, but to be of quantitative interest, it must pertain to a fairly large number.

The Clinton presidential campaign in 1992 seemed aware that there may be something to this theory. In campaign headquarters in Little Rock, Arkansas, James Carville hung up a sign that said, "It's the Economy, Stupid"—hence the title of this chapter.

The theory as presented so far is hard to test because we do not generally observe voters' expectations of their future well-being. We must add to the theory an assumption about what influences these expectations. We will assume that the recent performance of the economy at the time of the election influences voters' expectations of their own future well-being. If the economy has been doing well, voters take this as a positive sign about their future well-being under the incumbent party. Conversely, if the economy has been doing poorly, voters take this as a negative sign. The theory and this assumption then imply that when the economy is doing well, voters tend to vote for the incumbent party, and when the economy is doing poorly, they tend to vote for the opposition party.

We now have something that can be tested. Does the incumbent party tend to do well when the economy is good and poorly when the economy is bad? Let's begin by taking as the measure of how the economy is doing the growth rate of output per person (real per capita gross domestic product [GDP]) in the year of the election. Let's also use as the measure of how well the incumbent party does in an election the percentage of the two-party vote that it receives. For example, in 1996, the growth rate was 3.3 percent, and the incumbent party candidate (Bill Clinton) got 54.7 percent of the combined Democratic and Republican vote (and won—over Bob Dole). In 2008, the growth rate was –2.3 percent, and the incumbent party candidate (John McCain) got 46.3 percent of the combined two-party vote (and lost—to Barack Obama). (The reasons for using the two-party vote will be explained later.)

Figure 1-1 is a graph of the incumbent party vote share plotted against the growth rate for the 24 elections between 1916 and 2008. The incumbent party vote share is on the vertical axis, and the growth rate is on the horizontal axis. According to the above theory, there should be a positive relationship between the two: when the growth rate is high, the vote share should be high, and vice versa.

Vote Share (%)

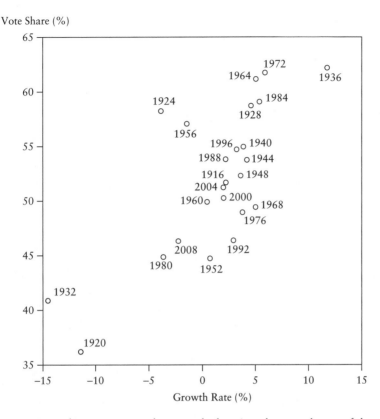

FIGURE **1-1** Incumbent party vote share graphed against the growth rate of the economy

Two observations that stand out in Figure 1-1 are the elections of 1932 and 1936. In 1932, the incumbent party's candidate (Herbert Hoover) got 40.9 percent of the two-party vote, a huge defeat in a year when the growth rate of the economy was –14.6 percent. (Yes, that's a minus sign!) In 1936, the incumbent party's candidate (Franklin Roosevelt) got 62.2 percent of the two-party vote, a huge victory in a year when the growth rate of the economy was an exceptionally strong 11.8 percent. (Although 1936 was in the decade of the Great Depression, the economy actually grew quite rapidly in that year.)

Figure 1-1 shows that there does appear to be a positive relationship between the growth rate in the year of the election and the incumbent vote share: the scatter of points has an upward pattern. Voters may thus take into account the state of the economy when deciding for whom to vote, as the theory says.

The growth rate is not, however, the only measure of how well the economy is doing. For example, inflation may also be of concern to voters. When inflation has been high under the incumbent party, a voter may fear that his or her income will not rise as fast as will prices in the future if the incumbent party's candidate is elected and thus that he or she will be worse off under the incumbent party. The voter may thus vote against the incumbent party. Many people consider inflation bad for their financial well-being, so high inflation may turn voters away from the incumbent party.

Deflation, which is falling prices, is also considered by many to be bad. People tend to like stable prices (that is, prices that on average don't change much from year to year). There have been some periods in U.S. history in which there was deflation. For example, prices on average declined during the four-year periods prior to the elections of 1924 and 1932. If voters dislike deflation as much as they dislike inflation, then inflation of −5 percent (which is deflation) is the same in the minds of the voters as inflation of +5 percent. Therefore, in dealing with the data on inflation, we will drop the minus sign when there is deflation. We are thus assuming that in terms of its impact on voters, a deflation of 5 percent is the same as an inflation of 5 percent.

To see how the incumbent party vote share and inflation (or deflation) are related, Figure 1-2 graphs the vote share against inflation for the 24 elections between 1916 and 2008. According to the theory just discussed, there should be a negative relationship between the two: when inflation is high, the vote share should be low, and vice versa. You can see from Figure 1-2 that there does seem to be at least a slight negative relationship between the incumbent party vote share and inflation: the scatter of points has a slight downward pattern.

We are not, however, limited to a choice between one or the other—the growth rate or inflation. It may be that *both* the growth rate and inflation affect voting behavior. In other words, we need not assume that voters look at only one aspect of the economy when they are considering their future financial well-being. For example, if both the growth rate and inflation are high, a voter may be less inclined to vote for

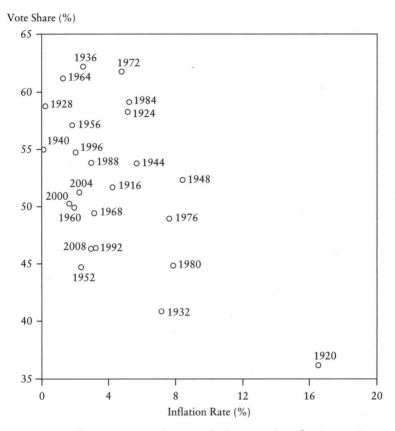

FIGURE **1-2** Incumbent party vote share graphed against the inflation rate

the incumbent party than if the growth rate is high and inflation is low. Similarly, if both the growth rate and inflation are low, a voter may be more inclined to vote for the incumbent party than if the growth rate is low and inflation is high.

An example of a high growth rate and low inflation is 1964, where the growth rate was about 5 percent and inflation was about 1 percent. In this case, the incumbent, President Johnson, won by a landslide over Barry Goldwater—receiving 61.2 percent of the two-party vote. An example of a low growth rate and high inflation is 1980, where the growth rate was about –4 percent and inflation about 8 percent. In this case, the

incumbent, President Carter, lost by a large amount to Ronald Reagan—
receiving only 44.8 percent of the two-party vote.

To carry on, we are also not limited to only two measures of the
economy. In addition to observing how the economy has grown in the
year of the election, voters may look at growth rates over the entire four
years of the administration. In other words, past growth rates *along with*
the growth rate in the election year may affect voting behavior. One measure of how good or bad past growth rates have been is the number of
quarters during the four-year period of the administration in which the
growth rate has exceeded some large number. These are quarters in which
the output news was particularly good, and voters may be inclined to
remember these kinds of events. There is some evidence from psychological experiments that people tend to remember peak stimuli more than
they remember average stimuli, a finding that is consistent with voters
remembering very strong growth quarters more than the others. Therefore, voters may be more inclined to vote for the incumbent party if there
were many of these "good news quarters" during the administration than
if there were few.

Noneconomic factors may also affect voting behavior. If the
president is running for reelection, he (or maybe she in the future) may
have a head start. He can perhaps use the power of the presidency to
gain media attention, control events, and so forth. He is also presum-
ably well known to voters, and so there may be less uncertainty in voters' minds regarding the future if he is reelected rather than if someone
new is elected. Voters who do not like uncertainty may thus be more
inclined to vote for the incumbent party if the president is a candidate
than otherwise.

It is also possible that voters get tired, or bored, with a party if it
has been in power for a long time, feeling that time has come for a change.
Therefore, the longer a party has been in power, the less inclined many
voters may be to keep it in power. The vote share may thus depend on a
measure of the duration of the incumbent party.

The theory of voting behavior that has just been presented can
be summarized in Box 1-1. The items in the box are called *variables*. A
variable is something that changes, or varies. For example, the vote share
is different for different elections; it varies across elections. Likewise, the
growth rate is different for different elections; it also varies. Both the vote
share and the growth rate are thus variables.

BOX **1-1**

vote share depends on:	
	growth rate
	inflation
	good news quarters
	president running
	duration

The variable to be explained—in this case, the vote share—is called the *dependent* variable. According to the theory, it "depends" on the other variables in the box. The other variables in the box—growth rate, inflation, good news quarters, president running, and duration—are called *independent* or *explanatory* variables. They help "explain" the dependent variable. The independent or explanatory variables are not themselves explained by the theory; they simply do the explaining.

The theory we have proposed may not, of course, capture well the way that voters actually behave. Maybe the economy plays no role. Maybe the vote share depends on a completely different set of factors—personality factors, foreign policy issues, social welfare issues, and so forth. We must collect data and test the theory.

The Data

To test the theory, we need data on past election outcomes and on what the economy was like for each election. We have already seen data on the vote share and the growth rate in Figure 1-1 and data on the vote share and inflation in Figure 1-2. Table 1-1 presents a more detailed picture of the data. The two-party vote share is presented for each election from 1916 to 2008, along with the growth rate, the inflation rate, the number of good news quarters, and a measure of duration.

(Regarding the poem at the beginning of this chapter, William Jennings Bryan was the Democratic Party candidate in 1896, 1900, and 1908. He was defeated in the first two campaigns by William McKinley and in the 1908 campaign by William H. Taft. These elections are not in the sample in Table 1-1, but economic topics played a key role in Bryan's campaigns. In the election of 1896, for example, he made his famous cross of gold speech: "You shall not press down upon the brow of

TABLE **1-1** Data used for explaining the outcome of presidential elections, 1916–2008

Year	Party in Power 1 = D −1 = R	President Running 1 = yes 0 = no	Election Outcome	Incumbent Vote Share (%)	Growth Rate (%)	Inflation Rate (%)	Good News Quarters	Duration Value	Democratic Vote Share (%)
1916	1	1	President Wilson (D) beat Hughes (R)	51.7	2.2	4.3	3	0.00	51.7
1920	1	0	Cox (D) lost to Harding (R)	36.1	−11.5	16.5	5	1.00	36.1
1924	−1	1	President Coolidge (R) beat Davis (D) and LaFollette	58.3	−3.9	5.2	10	0.00	41.7
1928	−1	0	Hoover (R) beat Smith (D)	58.8	4.6	0.2	7	1.00	41.2
1932	−1	1	President Hoover (R) lost to F. Roosevelt (D)	40.9	−14.6	7.2	4	1.25	59.1
1936	1	1	President F. Roosevelt (D) beat Landon (R)	62.2	11.8	2.5	9	0.00	62.2
1940	1	1	President F. Roosevelt (D) beat Willkie (R)	55.0	3.9	0.1	8	1.00	55.0
1944	1	1	President F. Roosevelt (D) beat Dewey (R)	53.8	4.2	5.7	14	1.25	53.8
1948	1	1	President Truman (D) beat Dewey (R)	52.3	3.6	8.4	5	1.50	52.3
1952	1	0	Stevenson (D) lost to Eisenhower (R)	44.7	0.7	2.3	7	1.75	44.7
1956	−1	1	President Eisenhower (R) beat Stevenson (D)	57.1	−1.5	1.9	5	0.00	42.9
1960	−1	0	Nixon (R) lost to Kennedy (D)	49.9	0.5	1.9	5	1.00	50.1
1964	1	1	President Johnson (D) beat Goldwater (R)	61.2	5.1	1.3	10	0.00	61.2
1968	1	0	Humphrey (D) lost to Nixon (R)	49.4	5.0	3.1	7	1.00	49.4
1972	−1	1	President Nixon (R) beat McGovern (D)	61.8	5.9	4.8	4	0.00	38.2

1976	−1	0	Ford (R) lost to Carter (D)	49.0	3.8	7.6	5	1.00	51.0
1980	1	1	President Carter (D) lost to Reagan (R)	44.8	−3.7	7.9	5	0.00	44.8
1984	−1	1	President Reagan (R) beat Mondale (D)	59.1	5.4	5.2	8	0.00	40.9
1988	−1	0	G. Bush (R) beat Dukakis (D)	53.8	2.2	3.0	4	1.00	46.2
1992	−1	1	President G. Bush (R) lost to Clinton (D)	46.4	2.9	3.3	2	1.25	53.6
1996	1	1	President Clinton (D) beat Dole (R)	54.7	3.3	2.0	4	0.00	54.7
2000	1	0	Gore (D) lost to G. W. Bush (R)	50.3	2.0	1.6	7	0.00	50.3
2004	−1	1	President G. W. Bush (R) beat Kerry (D)	51.2	2.0	2.2	1	0.00	48.8
2008	−1	0	McCain (R) lost to Obama (D)	46.3	−2.3	3.1	1	0.00	53.7

NOTE: See Chapter 3 for description of the data.

labor this crown of thorns, you shall not crucify mankind upon a cross of gold." The 1896 campaign in part pitted northeastern creditors against southern and western debtors. Bryan wanted the dollar to be backed by silver as well as gold, which would have put more money in circulation and led to lower interest rates, thus benefiting the South and West over the Northeast.)

The data in Table 1-1 are discussed in more detail in Chapter 3, and so only a few points about the data will be made now. As mentioned earlier, in the periods before the elections of 1924 and 1932, inflation was negative (that is, there was deflation). Positive values are, however, listed in Table 1-1, reflecting the assumption that voters dislike deflation as much as they dislike inflation. If the president is running for reelection, the word *President* precedes the name. A candidate who was elected vice president and became president during the administration was counted as the president running for reelection. (Gerald Ford was not counted because he was not elected vice president; he was appointed vice president after Spiro Agnew resigned.)

The duration variable in Table 1-1 has a value of 0.0 if the incumbent party has been in power only one term before the election. It has a value of 1.0 if the incumbent party has been in power two terms in a row, a value of 1.25 for three terms in a row, a value of 1.50 for four terms in a row, and a value of 1.75 for five terms in a row. We will use this variable in Chapter 3; it can be ignored for now.

Because we are taking the vote share to be the share of the *two-party* vote, we are ignoring possible third-party influences. We are in effect assuming that third-party votes are taken roughly equally from the two major parties. Again, we will come back to this in Chapter 3.

Table 1-1 gives a good picture of what is to be explained and the variables that the theory says may be important in the explanation. In the election of 1916, the incumbent party was Democratic, and President Wilson beat the Republican Hughes with 51.7 percent of the two-party vote. The growth rate was 2.2 percent, and inflation was 4.3 percent. In 1920, the incumbent party was Democratic and the Democrat Cox lost to the Republican Harding by a landslide. Cox got only 36.1 percent of the two-party vote. For this election, the growth rate was –11.5 percent and inflation was 16.5 percent—hardly a good economy! This outcome is, of course, consistent with the theory: the economy was very poor, and the incumbent party got trounced.

You may want to go through the rest of the elections and see what the story is for each. Only three more will be mentioned here. As we noted above, in 1980 President Carter lost to Reagan with a vote share of 44.8 percent. The economy was not good for Carter—the growth rate was –3.7 percent and inflation was 7.9 percent. This outcome is again consistent with the theory. On the other hand, the theory has trouble with the 1992 election, when President G. Bush lost to Clinton with a vote share of 46.4 percent. Unlike 1980, the economy was not that bad in 1992—the growth rate was 2.9 percent and inflation was 3.3 percent. There is thus a puzzle as to why President G. Bush lost, or at least why he lost by as much as he did. We will return to this question in Chapter 3. In 2008, the incumbent party was Republican and the Republican John McCain lost to Democrat Barack Obama with a vote share of 46.3 percent. The economy was not good in 2008 regarding the growth rate, which was –2.3 percent.

On to the Tools

We have presented a theory of voting behavior in this chapter, and we have presented data that can be used to test the theory. This is, however, as far as we can go without the tools, and so it is on to Chapter 2. Once the tools have been explained in Chapter 2, they will be used in Chapter 3 to test the theory of voting behavior and to predict the 2012 election.

Plato, despair!
We prove by norms
How numbers bear
Empiric forms,

How random wrong
Will average right
If time be long
And error slight,

But in our hearts
Hyperbole
Curves and departs
To infinity.

Error is boundless.
Nor hope nor doubt,
Though both be groundless,
Will average out.

J. V. Cunningham, Meditation on Statistical Method

(Monday) Lesson 1: Begin with a Theory

We begin with a theory of what we are trying to explain. In the previous chapter, a theory of voting behavior was presented—a theory of what motivates people to vote the way they do. Although it does not matter where a theory comes from, it should have a ring of plausibility. A theory that seems completely at odds with how something works is not of much interest to test and is not likely to get us very far.

We are also interested in causation, not correlation. Two variables are positively correlated if large values of one are associated with large values of the other and small values of one are associated with small values of the other. (Two variables are negatively correlated if large values of one are associated with small values of the other and small values of one are associated with large values of the other.) If you look across cities, you will likely find that those with a relatively high percentage of air conditioners also have a relatively high percentage of people with skin cancer. Air conditioners and skin cancer are positively correlated across cities. But this does not mean that air conditioners cause skin cancer or that skin cancer causes people to buy air conditioners. In this case, the climate of a city is causing both. A theory is a statement that one or more variables cause another variable—the variable we are interested in explaining. A statement that air conditioners cause skin cancer is not a theory, or at least not a theory that is interesting to test, because it confuses correlation with causation.

It is easiest to explain the following tools using a particular theory as an example, and we will use the theory of voting behavior. To begin, we simplify matters and assume that the vote share depends only on the economy's growth rate in the year of the election. The theory we begin with is that the growth rate has a positive effect on the incumbent party vote share.

(Tuesday) Lesson 2: Collect Data

Empirical evidence or information is needed to test a theory. This requires collecting observations on the variable to be explained (the dependent variable) and the variables that, according to the theory, do the explaining (the independent or explanatory variables). Observations on variables are called *data*. Table 1-1 provides a good example of data collection. Observations are available for the period 1916–2008 on the vote share, the growth rate, and a number of other variables. This table contains the data that we will use to test the theory of voting behavior.

Data collection is perhaps the most important step in testing a theory. A good test requires that the variables for which observations are collected match closely the variables that the theory is talking about. It is not always easy to find good matches, and much of social science research consists of the nitty-gritty job of finding appropriate data. Tuesday is thus a critical day. Always keep in mind when deciding how much to trust the results of a test that a test is no better than the data behind it.

(Wednesday) Lesson 3: Fit the Data

This is the hardest lesson except for Lesson 4. If you have not worked this kind of material before—essentially fitting points to a line—you may need to go through it more than once. Keep in mind that the main aim of this lesson is to fit as closely as possible the theory from Lesson 1 to the data from Lesson 2.

We begin with Table 1-1, where we have 24 observations on the vote share and on the growth rate. In Figure 2-1, the vote share is graphed

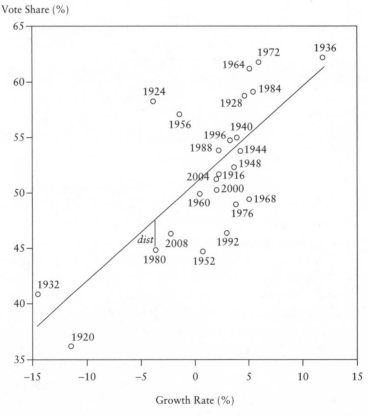

FIGURE **2-1**   Incumbent party vote share graphed against the growth rate of the economy

against the growth rate. This is the same graph as Figure 1-1, although now we are going to do more with it. The vote share is on the vertical axis, and the growth rate is on the horizontal axis.

Note that the points in Figure 2-1 have an upward pattern (rising from left to right). In other words, the vote share tends to be larger when the growth rate is larger. This is, of course, exactly what our theory says should be the case. In some cases, however, one vote share is larger than another, even though it has a smaller growth rate associated with it. For example, the vote share for 1956 is larger than the vote share for 1996, even though the growth rate for 1956 is smaller than that for 1996. It is clear that the points in the figure do not all lie on a straight line, and in this sense, the relationship between the vote share and the growth rate is not exact.

Even though all the points in Figure 2-1 do not lie on a straight line, we can ask which straight line the points are closest to. Put another way, we can ask which line best "fits" the points. To see what is involved in finding the best fitting line, consider drawing some line through the points, such as the line drawn in the figure. You should think for now of this line as being any arbitrary line, not necessarily the best fitting line. Some points on the particular line in the figure, such as the one for 1940, are almost exactly on the line. Others, such as the one for 1920, are farther away from the line. The vertical distance between a point and the line, such as that labeled *dist* for 1980, is a measure of how far the point is from the line. This distance is sometimes called an *error*. If all points were exactly on the line, all errors would be zero, and the relationship between the vote share and the growth rate would be exact. Otherwise, the larger the distances are on average, the less precise is the relationship.

If we define an error as the difference between the point on the line and the actual point, then errors corresponding to the points below the line are positive, and errors corresponding to the points above the line are negative. Now, if we change the sign of the negative errors to positive and add up all the errors, the answer (the sum) is a measure of how closely the line fits the points. We are just adding up all the distances of the points from the line. One line can be said to fit better than another line if it has a smaller sum. In practice, a more popular way of measuring how well a line fits the points is first to take each error and square it (that is, multiply each error by itself) and then to add up all the squared errors. Either way, the general idea is the same. In terms of deciding which line fits best, a line in which the points are far from the line (that is, when the distances from the points to the line are large) is not as good as a line in which the points are close to the line.

We will follow the convention of squaring the errors before summing them. Now, imagine drawing thousands of straight lines in Figure 2-1, each with a different position in the figure, and for each line taking the 24 errors, squaring them, and then adding up the squared errors. We can thus associate one number (the sum of the errors squared) with each line, and this number is a measure of how well that particular line fits the points. If the number for a given line is large relative to numbers for other lines, this means that the given line is not positioned well in the figure. For this line, the distances from the points to the line are on average large, so the line does not fit the points well. The best fitting line out of the thousands of lines is simply the line with the smallest number (that is, the smallest sum of squared errors). Although it would take hours to draw thousands of lines by hand and compute the number for each line, computers can find the best fitting line very quickly. It takes almost no time for a computer to find the line with the smallest sum of squared errors.

Assume that we have found the best fitting line with the help of a computer. (This is in fact the line drawn in Figure 2-1.) Associated with this line is, of course, its sum of squared errors. Although the sum of squared errors is a measure of how well the line fits the points, it does not give a sense of what a typical error is. A better sense of the size of a typical error can be obtained by dividing the sum of squared errors by the number of observations, which gives the average squared error, and then taking the square root of the average squared error, which gives the average error. It turns out, for example, that the sum of squared errors for the line in Figure 2-1 is 486.9. If we divide this number by 24, the number of points in the figure, we get 20.3, which is the average squared error. If we then take the square root of this number, we get 4.5, which is the average error.

Although we might use the average error of 4.5 as the measure of a typical error, in practice a slightly different measure is used. In the present example, instead of dividing the sum of squared errors of 486.9 by 24, we divide it by 22. In other words, we subtract 2 from the number of points before dividing. We use 2 because the line is determined by two points.

If there were only 2 points in Figure 2-1, the line would fit perfectly—2 zero errors. So we start off in this sense with 2 zero errors, leaving 22 to play with. If we divide 486.9 by 22, we get 22.1. The square root of this number is 4.7, slightly larger than 4.5. We then take 4.7 as the measure of a typical error. This error measure is sometimes called a *standard error*, and we will use this terminology. A standard error is just a measure of the average size of a typical error for a line like that in Figure 2-1.

Is the standard error of 4.7 for the line in Figure 2-1 large or small? We can see from Table 1-1 in the previous chapter that the vote share ranges from a low of 36.1 percent in 1920 to a high of 62.2 percent in 1936. The difference between the high and the low is thus 26.1, and so 4.7 is fairly small compared to this range. On the other hand, many elections have been decided with a margin less than 4.7 percentage points, and so on this score, 4.7 is fairly large. We will see in the next chapter that when the other explanatory variables are taken into account, the standard error is in fact much smaller than 4.7. For now, however, we will stay with using only the growth rate and thus the standard error of 4.7.

We have so far found the best fitting line and calculated the standard error. Another way to get a sense of how well the line fits the points is simply to examine individual points. In particular, it is of interest to see which points are far from the line (that is, which points have large errors associated with them). For example, the error for the election of 1924 is quite large, as we can see in Figure 2-1. For this election, the vote share is high, and the growth rate is low (in fact negative), resulting in a point far above the line. The election of 1956 is a similar case, where the vote share is high, and the growth rate is low. A point that is fairly far below the line is 1952, where the vote share is low, and the growth rate is modest. On the other hand, a number of points—such as 1936, 1940, 1944, and 1988—are very close to the line.

Another useful number we can get from Figure 2-1 is the *slope* of the line. The slope of a line is the measure of how steep it is. The slope of the line in Figure 2-1 is positive: it rises upward and to the right. A negative slope is one in which the line moves downward and to the right. The slope of the line in Figure 2-1 is 0.9. This means that if you move along the horizontal axis by 1 unit, the vote share on the line will increase by 0.9 units. For example, an increase in the growth rate of 1.0 percentage point will increase the vote share by 0.9 percentage points on the line.

You can probably see already why the size of the slope is important. If the slope is large (that is, the line is steep), the growth rate has a large effect on the vote share according to the line. If, on the other hand, the slope is zero (that is, the line is horizontal), the growth rate has no effect on the vote share according to the line. Clearly, if the slope in Figure 2-1 were zero or close to zero, there would be no support for the theory that the growth rate affects the vote share.

The slope of the best fitting line is sometimes called the *estimated slope*, and we will use this terminology. The slope is estimated in the sense that it is computed by finding the best fitting line given whatever observations are at our disposal.

This is it for Lesson 3. The basic idea is to see how well a theory fits the data. In the simple case considered so far of a dependent variable and one explanatory variable, the theory is used to choose the two variables (in our example, the vote share and the growth rate). The data are then used to find the best fitting line. The main point of this lesson is to show how best fitting lines are found.

(Thursday) Lesson 4: Test

Just because we have found the best fitting line does not mean we have discovered anything interesting or useful. One of the main issues social scientists worry about when analyzing relationships such as the one between the vote share and the growth rate is that a relationship may have been uncovered by coincidence and that it is in fact not truly valid. In the present example, we worry that the vote share is not really affected by the growth rate even though for the 24 observations it looks like it is.

One way to express our anxiety is by stating our concern that the slope of the true line in a figure like Figure 2-1 is zero. If the true slope is zero, there is no relationship between the growth rate and the vote share. Although the slope of the line in Figure 2-1 is positive, as the theory of voting behavior says it should be, perhaps the positive slope is just a fluke. It may be just by chance that the 24 available observations (points) show a positive effect. If we had 24 other observations (say by waiting for 24 more elections to take place), they might show a much smaller positive slope or even a negative slope. We need to test whether the positive slope is or is not a fluke.

The main point of this lesson is to explain how we can test whether the true slope is zero. As noted at the end of Lesson 3, the slope in Figure 2-1 is 0.9, and we want to see how likely it is that the true slope is zero, even though we have estimated it to be 0.9. We will show that we can compute for an estimated slope its *t-statistic*. We will then see that if the value of the *t*-statistic is greater than about 2.0, it is very unlikely that the true slope is zero. A *t*-statistic greater than 2.0 is thus good for the theory. It says that the slope we have estimated by finding the best fitting line is unlikely to be truly zero.

The rest of this lesson is difficult, and if you are willing to take the result about the *t*-statistic on faith, you may skip to Lesson 5. Or you may skip this material for now and come back later, once you have seen, in Chapters 3 and beyond, the use of *t*-statistics in action.

Thursday Morning

We begin with the errors in Figure 2-1. Remember that an error for a point is the distance from the point to the line. Also remember that an error is negative if the point is below the line and positive if the point is above the line. Now, say that instead of 24 errors, we had hundreds of them (from hundreds of elections), and we recorded how many of them were between 0.0 and 0.1, how many were between 0.1 and 0.2, how many were between −0.1 and 0.0, and so on. In other words, suppose we have intervals of size 0.1 and we record how many errors are in each interval: we record how many very small errors there are, how many fairly small errors, how many medium errors, and so on.

In most cases, we will find that there are more very small errors than small ones, more small errors than medium errors, more medium errors than large ones, and so on. In fact, in many cases, if we graph the number of errors in each interval against the position of the interval on the horizontal axis, we will get points that lie on a curve that is approximately like that in Figure 2-2. The curve in Figure 2-2 is a bell-shaped curve, which is a curve you may have seen in other contexts. If, for example, you divided scores on intelligence tests (IQ scores) into small intervals and graphed the number of scores in each interval against the position of the interval on the horizontal axis, you would get points that lie approximately on a bell-shaped curve.

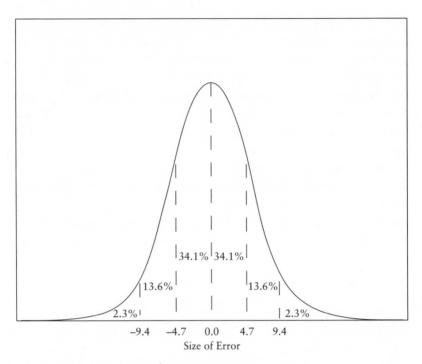

FIGURE **2-2**   Bell-shaped curve for errors in Figure 2.1

We will assume that the curve in Figure 2-2 is an exact bell-shaped curve. We will also assume that the peak of the bell-shaped curve corresponds to an error of zero and that the standard error is, as computed in Lesson 3, 4.7. A bell-shaped curve has some useful characteristics concerning the size of the area under the curve that we need to know about. The total area under the curve is the space under the curve and above the horizontal axis. Consider starting from zero and moving a distance of 4.7 to the right and 4.7 to the left, where 4.7 is the standard error. Doing this sweeps out 34.1 percent of the area to the right of zero and 34.1 percent of the area to the left of zero, for a total of 68.2 percent of the area under the curve. This area is shown in Figure 2-2. In other words, 68.2 percent of the errors are between –4.7 and 4.7, where again 4.7 is the standard error.

If we sweep out the area between 4.7 and 9.4, we get another 13.6 percent, and if we sweep out the area between –4.7 and –9.4, we get another 13.6 percent. The total area between −9.4 and 9.4 is thus 95.4 percent. Looked at another way, the area to the right of 9.4 is 2.3 percent and the area to the left of −9.4 is 2.3 percent. That is, for a bell-shaped curve with a standard error of 4.7, only 2.3 percent of the errors are larger than 9.4 and only 2.3 percent are smaller than −9.4.

So, you might ask, why are you telling me this? In particular, what does this have to do with the question of whether the positive slope in Figure 2-1 is a fluke? Well, we are making progress, but patience is still needed. The next step is to consider the following thought experiment. Imagine there is another universe in which the true relationship between the vote share and the growth rate is the line in Figure 2-1 (slope equal to 0.9). Imagine also that in this universe there are 24 presidential elections with the same 24 growth rates as in Figure 2-1. For our thought experiment, we want this universe to have different errors than the errors depicted in Figure 2-1.

Consider, for example, the 1992 election, when President George H. W. Bush lost to candidate Bill Clinton. As in any election, there were many things that affected voting behavior aside from the growth rate, and for this election, these other things were a net negative for Bush. This can be seen by noting that the point for 1992 in Figure 2-1 is below the line. Remember that the distance from a point to the line is the error for that point. Because the point for 1992 is below the line, the error is positive (the difference between the point on the line and the actual point). Although not directly recorded in Figure 2-1, the error for 1992 is 7.1 percent, which is fairly large. In 1992, President Bush got 46.4 percent of the two-party vote, which is the 1992 point in Figure 2-1. The position on the line corresponding to the 1992 growth rate is 53.5 percent. The 7.1 error is the difference between 46.4 and 53.5. In the present context, we can look upon an error in any given election as reflecting all the other things that affect voting behavior aside from the growth rate. The more these other things matter, the larger on average will the error be. We have, fortunately, a measure of how large the errors are on average, which is the standard error of 4.7.

Now comes the key step. We want to draw for the other universe a different error for the 1992 election from the one that actually occurred (which was 7.1). We are going to draw this error from a bell-shaped curve with a standard error of 4.7. This error will in general be different from the actual error of 7.1. We are imagining an election in 1992 in the other universe with the same growth rate but a different set of the other things that affect voting behavior. Maybe in the other universe Clinton did very poorly in the debates, leading fewer people to vote for him. Or maybe President Bush successfully toppled Saddam Hussein in the Gulf War, leading more people to vote for him. We are thus imagining a different set of other things, which implies a different error, and we are drawing this error at random from a bell-shaped curve with a standard error of 4.7. By using a standard error of 4.7, we are assuming that the same bell-shaped curve pertains to the other universe as it pertains to ours. In other words, the average size of the effect of the "other things" is assumed to be the same.

Say we drew an error of 3.0 for 1992. What would be the actual vote share in this case? Remember we are assuming the line in Figure 2-1 is correct, and given the growth rate for 1992, the point of the line for 1992 is 53.5, as noted above. For the actual error of 7.1, the actual vote share is 46.4, which is simply 53.5 minus 7.1. If instead we have an error of 3.0, the actual vote share is 53.5 minus 3.0, or 50.5. In this other universe, the vote share for President Bush is larger than it is in the actual universe because the error is smaller. To get the vote share in the other universe, we thus take the point on the line in Figure 2-1, which we are assuming is correct, and subtract the error that we draw.

We draw an error not only for 1992, but for the other 23 elections as well, each time using the bell-shaped curve with a standard error of 4.7. From these 23 errors, we can get 23 vote-share values as just discussed. This means that we have 24 different points (vote shares) in Figure 2-1. Using these new points, we can find the line that best fits the points. Because the points are different, the best fitting line will generally be in a different position from the line in Figure 2-1. So generally, it will have a different slope. The slope in the other universe will generally not be 0.9.

We now go to another universe and draw a new set of 24 errors. We get a new set of vote-share values, again assuming that the line in Figure 2-1 is correct, and we find the best fitting line for the new vote-share values. This gives us another slope. We keep doing this until we have run through many universes, say 1,000. We have thus computed 1,000 different estimated slopes.

The next step is to examine the 1,000 slopes. As we did above for the errors, we divide these slopes into small intervals and then graph the

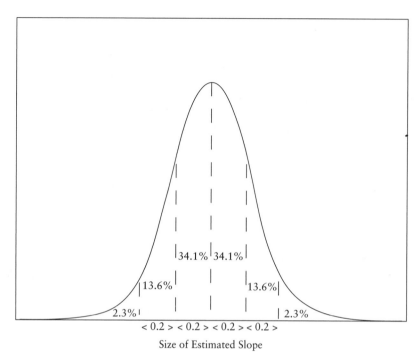

FIGURE **2-3** Bell-shaped curve for estimated slopes

number of slopes in each interval against the position of the interval on the horizontal axis. When we do this, we get points that lie approximately on a bell-shaped curve. This curve is drawn in Figure 2-3. We will assume that this curve is exactly bell-shaped. In practice, it is not quite bell-shaped, but for most applications, the bell-shaped curve is a very close approximation.

It is important to keep in mind that we have moved from errors to slopes. The bell-shaped curve in Figure 2-2 is for the errors from Figure 2-1 (that is, the distances from the points to the line), whereas the bell-shaped curve in Figure 2-3 is for the slopes we have estimated from our different universes.

We use the bell-shaped curve in Figure 2-3 in the following way. We start from the estimated slope that is exactly under the peak of the curve, and we sweep out 34.1 percent of the area to the right. We know from the characteristic of a bell-shaped curve that the distance we travel along the horizontal axis to sweep out 34.1 percent of the area is one standard error. In the present example, this distance turns out to be 0.2. This means that the standard error of the estimated slope is 0.2. As shown in the figure, if we move another 0.2 to the right, we sweep out 13.6 percent of the area. If we move left from the center by 0.2, we sweep out 34.1 percent of the area, and if we move left another 0.2, we sweep out another 13.6 percent of the area.

This standard error of 0.2 for the estimated slope in Figure 2-3 is, of course, different from the standard error of 4.7 in Figure 2-2, which is for the line in Figure 2-1. Each bell-shaped curve has its own standard error. We always need to be clear in what follows as to which standard error we are talking about. When there is possible confusion, we will use the phrases *standard error of the line* and *standard error of the estimated slope*.

Let us recap what we have done so far. We have assumed that the line in Figure 2-1 is correct, and using it and the bell-shaped curve in Figure 2-2, we have generated many sets of 24 vote shares by drawing errors. For each set of 24 vote shares, we have found the best fitting line, which gives us an estimated slope. Once we have computed many slope values, we use the bell-shaped curve in Figure 2-3 to find the standard error of the estimated slope. All the work so far has simply been to compute the standard error of the estimated slope. In practice, this standard error can be computed in a way that does not require drawing errors from hypothetical universes, but the answer is the same in either case.

We still have one more key step to take, but you may want to take a break for lunch before finishing. You should have a good idea of what the standard error of the estimated slope is before reading further.

Thursday Afternoon

The main issue we are worried about from the point of view of the theory of voting behavior is whether the true slope in Figure 2-1 is zero. If the slope is truly zero, it means the growth rate has no effect on the vote share: changes in the growth rate have no effect on the vote share if the line is completely flat. If the slope is zero, then the theory is not supported by the data.

Fortunately, we can now test whether the slope is zero. This is done in Figure 2-4. The figure is based on the assumption that the true slope is zero. We know from Figure 2-1 that the slope we have computed is 0.9. To test whether 0.9 is a fluke, we need to know the chance that we would get a value of 0.9 if the true slope were zero. This is where we need our standard error of the estimated slope of 0.2. Figure 2-4 shows it is very unlikely with a standard error of 0.2 that we would get an estimated slope of 0.9 if the true slope were zero. The probability that we would get a slope of 0.9 if the true slope were zero is the area under the curve to the right of 0.9 in the figure, which is very close to zero. (The area is so small that it can't even be seen in the figure!) The data thus support the theory that the growth rate affects the vote share. To repeat, if the growth rate did not affect the vote share, it is unlikely we would get a slope of 0.9 in Figure 2-1. It is thus likely that the theory is true.

Now comes the punch line. If we divide the slope (0.9) by the standard error of the estimated slope (0.2), we get what is called a *t-statistic* (4.5 in this example). The *t*-statistic is a highly useful concept. Assume

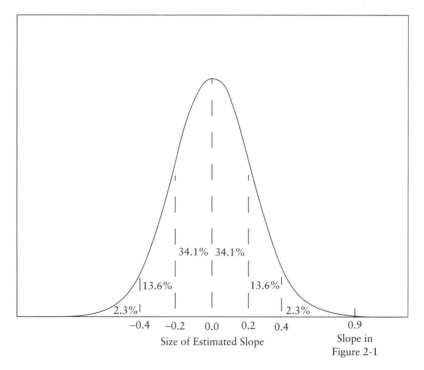

FIGURE **2-4**   Bell-shaped curve for estimated slopes if true slope were zero

for the sake of argument that we had an estimated slope of 0.4 instead of 0.9 with the same standard error of 0.2. This would mean that the *t*-statistic is 2.0. We can see from Figure 2-4 that for an estimated slope of 0.4, 2.3 percent of the area under the curve lies to the right of 0.4. Therefore, the probability that we would get a slope of 0.4 if the true slope were zero (and the standard error of the estimated slope were 0.2) is just 2.3 percent. For a *t*-statistic of 2.0, it is thus unlikely that the true slope is zero and thus likely that the theory is true. In practice, a *t*-statistic of 2.0, or around 2.0, is used as a cutoff regarding whether a theory is supported or not supported. A theory is not supported if the *t*-statistic is less than 2.0 or thereabouts, and a theory is supported if the *t*-statistic is greater than 2.0 or thereabouts. This convention is, of course, somewhat arbitrary, and other cutoffs could be used. If a *t*-statistic less than 2.0 were used as a cutoff, more theories would be supported, and if a *t*-statistic greater than 2.0 were used as a cutoff, fewer theories would be supported. We will use a cutoff of 2.0 in this book.

If a slope is negative, the *t*-statistic is negative. In this case, the cutoff is a *t*-statistic of –2.0. A *t*-statistic less than –2.0 (such as –3.0) means it is unlikely that the true slope is zero; thus, a theory stating that the slope were negative would be supported when the *t*-statistic is less than –2.0.

Using a cutoff of 2.0 (or –2.0), an estimated slope is said to be *significant* if it has a *t*-statistic greater than 2.0 (or less than –2.0). Significant means it is unlikely that the true slope is zero. Significant is also used sometimes to refer to a variable that has a significant estimated slope. In our present example, the growth rate is significant because the *t*-statistic of the estimated slope is 4.5, which is greater than the cutoff of 2.0. The results are summarized in Box 2-1. The estimated slope of the line is 0.9, and it has a *t*-statistic of 4.5. Since the *t*-statistic is greater than 2.0, we can say that the growth rate is significant. The standard error of the line, a measure of a typical error, is 4.7, and there are 24 points, or observations.

BOX **2-1**

vote share depends on:		*t*-statistic
0.9	growth rate	4.5
50.9	intercept	51.4
standard error: 4.7		
number of observations: 24		

The term in the box that we have not yet discussed is the *intercept*. The line in Figure 2-1 has both a slope and an intercept. The intercept is the point on the line where the growth rate is zero. When we find the best fitting line, we find both its slope and its intercept. The intercept has a standard error associated with it just like the slope does, and its standard error can be computed in the same way as was done for the slope's standard error. Once the intercept's standard error is computed, its *t*-statistic can be computed. As can be seen in the box, the *t*-statistic of the intercept is 51.4, which is huge. Not surprisingly, the data strongly reject the case that the true intercept is zero. The intercept is 50.9, which means that if the growth rate were zero, the vote share would be 50.9 percent according to the line. The line thus says that the incumbent party wins by a small margin if the growth rate is zero.

As a final point, it is important to see how the size of a *t*-statistic is related to the size of the standard error of the line, both of which are presented in Box 2-1. Consider, for example, a case in which the points in Figure 2-1 lie on average much closer to the line than is actually the case in the figure. In particular, say that the size of a typical error (that is, the standard error of the line) is 1.7 rather than 4.7. This means that the bell-shaped curve in Figure 2-2 is much less spread out. Now, when we are computing the standard error of the estimated slope by drawing many sets of 24 errors (from many universes), the errors are on average smaller. With smaller errors, the computed vote-share values are closer to the line in Figure 2-1. The best fitting line using the new values will thus be closer to the line in Figure 2-1, and so the estimated slope will be closer to 0.9. In other words, the estimated slopes will vary less when the errors that are drawn are smaller, and so the standard error of the estimated slope will be smaller (Figure 2-3 will be less spread out). Therefore, the *t*-statistic of the slope will be larger. This, of course, makes sense. If the errors in Figure 2-1 are on average small, we have more confidence that the slope is not a fluke than if the errors are on average large.

If a slope has a *t*-statistic that is very large in absolute value— much larger than 2.0—it is sometimes said to be *highly significant*. It is also sometimes said to be *precisely estimated*.

We are finally finished with Lesson 4. We have shown how to test whether the true slope of a line is zero given the slope that was computed by finding the best fitting line. The test is to compute the *t*-statistic of the estimated slope and see if it is greater than 2.0 or less than –2.0. If it is, then it is unlikely that the true slope is zero, which is support for the theory. One should not, however, get carried away with this result. The test is not necessarily the final answer, which is the subject matter of Lesson 5.

(Friday) Lesson 5: Think About Pitfalls

Since the t-statistic for the growth rate in our example is much greater than 2.0, are we almost positive that the growth rate affects the vote share? Figure 2-4 would suggest yes because there is a very small probability that we would get a slope of 0.9 if the true slope were zero. Alas, life is not quite this simple. Mistakes are possible that would not be caught by the test using the t-statistic. The theory may be wrong even with a t-statistic of 4.5. The following are possible pitfalls that you need to be aware of even with large t-statistics.

Perhaps the truth is that what affects the vote share is not the growth rate but the size of the armed forces. The size of the armed forces is large during wars, and if people rally around the flag during wars, they may be more inclined to vote for the incumbent party during wars than otherwise. Wars also tend to stimulate the economy, and so the growth rate is on average higher during wars than at other times. The growth rate and the size of the armed forces thus tend to move together: when one is high, the other tends to be high, and when one is low, the other tends to be low. (The growth rate and the size of the armed forces are positively correlated.) If this is true, then high growth rates will be associated with large vote shares and low growth rates will be associated with small vote shares. We may thus get a pattern of points like that in Figure 2-1 (namely, an upward pattern), but what is really affecting the vote share is not the growth rate but the size of the armed forces. We would be fooling ourselves in thinking that the growth rate is the cause. We thus have to be careful that the variable we think is affecting the vote share is not in fact acting as a proxy for something else.

It is also possible that *both* the growth rate and the size of the armed forces affect the vote share. In other words, there may be both a rally-around-the-flag effect and a separate growth-rate effect. We discuss how to treat two explanatory variables instead of just one later in this chapter. What we can say now is that if both variables matter but only the growth rate is included, the growth rate will get too much credit regarding its effect on the vote share. The estimated slope will be too large because by omitting the size of the armed forces, the growth rate is picking up part of the effect of the size of the armed forces on the vote share. This problem is called *omitted variable bias*. The estimated slope for an explanatory variable is wrong (biased) because some other explanatory variable has been omitted that truly affects the dependent variable and that is also correlated with the included explanatory variable.

The use of polling results provides a good example of another possible pitfall. Say that for each election one had polling data one week before the election. If in a figure like Figure 2-1 one graphed the vote share against the polling results, there is likely to be an upward pattern and fairly small errors on average around the best fitting line. Polls are usually fairly accurate one week before the election. The slope of the best fitting line is likely to be positive and have a large *t*-statistic. It is not the case, however, that the polling results are *causing* the voters to vote the way they do. The polls are just asking voters one week ahead how they are going to vote. Therefore, good fits and large *t*-statistics do not guarantee that one has explained anything. There can be correlation without causation.

Another possible pitfall is that voting behavior may have changed sometime during the period of the data. Possibly, the true slope was large during the 1916–1944 period and small (perhaps zero) after that. The best fitting line in Figure 2-1 would be based on the incorrect assumption that the true slope is the same for both periods. Although this mistake will make the average error larger than it would be if there were no shift of behavior, the *t*-statistic for the estimated slope may still turn out to be greater than 2.0. Possible shifting behavior is a nightmare for social scientists trying to explain behavior over time because stability is needed to learn very much.

It is also possible that the true relationship is not a straight line in Figure 2-1 but a curved line. Maybe the line begins to curve up at a growth rate of about 5 percent. Incorrectly using a straight line may still result in a positive estimated slope and a *t*-statistic greater than 2.0.

Another interesting way we might be fooled goes under the name of *data mining*. Say that we have observations on 100 possible variables that we think may affect the vote share. We then try each variable, one by one, and see what its estimated slope and *t*-statistic are. Let's say we then pick the variable with the largest t-statistic and conclude that this variable affects the vote share. The potential problem with this procedure should be obvious. By trying so many variables, it is likely that just by chance we have found one that results in a good fit and an estimated slope with a t-statistic greater than 2.0. In other words, even if none of the 100 variables truly affect the vote share, we may find some that by chance fit well.

There are two ways to mitigate the data mining problem. One is to use theory to reduce the number of variables to try. Stupid variables, such as a candidate's eye color, can be eliminated. We can use theory to narrow the list of possible variables to those that have some plausibility. The other way concerns prediction, which is the topic of Lesson 7.

To conclude, one must take any t-statistic with a grain of salt. High t-statistics are not a guarantee of success, and any result must be examined carefully for possible pitfalls.

(Saturday) Lesson 6: Examine the Results

If the tests of a theory reveal that the data do not support it, then this lesson and the next are of no interest. It is of no interest to examine results like the size of the slope or to use the slope to make predictions if the theory is not supported. Similarly, if the possible pitfalls seem really serious, we may not want to continue even if the theory were supported using the tests in Lesson 4. We need to have some confidence in the theory before we can use it.

If the results support a theory and the possible pitfalls do not seem serious, the next step is to examine the implications of the results. In Figure 2-1, for example, it is of interest to see what the line says about the size of the effect of the growth rate on the vote share. If, say, the growth rate increases from 2.0 percent to 3.0 percent, how much does the line say the vote share should increase? We have already answered this question in our discussion of the slope at the end of Lesson 3. The size of the effect is measured by the slope of the line. A steep slope implies a much larger effect than does a mild slope. The slope of the line in Figure 2-1 is 0.9. The line thus tells us that if the growth rate increases by 1.0, the vote share should increase by 0.9. If the slope were instead steeper, say 1.5, then an increase in the growth rate of 1.0 would mean that the vote share should increase by 1.5.

A slope of 0.9 is fairly large in the context of this example. For instance, it can be seen in Table 1-1 in Chapter 1 that the growth rate was −3.7 in 1980 and 5.4 in 1984, which is a difference of 9.1. A change in the growth rate of 9.1 implies, according to the line, that the vote share should change by 0.9 times 9.1, or 8.2, which is a large change in the vote share. It is interesting to note that the actual vote share was 44.8 percent in 1980 (President Carter lost to Reagan) and 59.1 percent in 1984 (President Reagan beat Mondale), a difference of 14.3. The actual change in the vote share was thus larger than 8.2 implied by the line, but the line got quite a bit of the increase.

In our simple example here, all we really have to examine is the size of the slope, which we have done. In most applications, there is more to be done (that is, more implications of the results to consider). We will see examples in the following chapters.

(Sunday) Lesson 7: Predict

Once we have done all the above work, prediction is easy and fun. We must not get too excited, however. The possible pitfalls we discussed in Lesson 5 are always lurking in the shadows, and we must not become overconfident.

Say that we want to use the line in Figure 2-1 to predict the 2012 election, which was not one of the 24 observations (the last election used was 2008). To make a prediction, we must first choose a value for the growth rate. Suppose we are making a prediction in January 2012, and we think the growth rate in 2012 will be 3.0 percent. We know, from Box 2-1, that the intercept is 50.9. This means that the value of the vote share on the line at a growth rate of 0.0 is 50.9. How much will the vote share increase if the growth rate is 3.0 rather than 0.0? Since the slope is 0.9, the vote share increases by 0.9 times 3.0, or 2.7. The vote share on the line at a growth rate of 3.0 is thus 50.9 plus 2.7, or 53.6. The incumbent party (Democratic) is thus predicted to win with 53.6 percent of the vote for a growth rate of 3.0 percent.

Say instead you thought in January 2012 that there was going to be a recession in 2012, and the growth rate was going to be −3.0. In this case, the predicted vote share is 50.9 minus 2.7, or 48.2, which would mean a Republican victory.

It is thus easy to make a prediction. Pick a growth rate, and find out where on the line in Figure 2-1 you are for this growth rate. Note that any prediction assumes that the error for 2012 will be zero (that is, the vote share will be exactly on the line). This is where one needs to be cautious. A typical error is 4.7 (the standard error of the line), so the actual outcome could differ from the predicted value by quite a bit. The standard error of 4.7 incorporates all the factors that affect voting behavior other than the growth rate, and these other factors have on average an effect of 4.7 on the vote share. You can see from Figure 2-2 that 68.2 percent of the time the error will be between –4.7 and 4.7. So with a predicted vote share of 53.6 percent, we can say that 68.2 percent of the time the actual vote share will be between 48.9 and 58.3 percent. This is, of course, a fairly wide range. (We will see in the next chapter that the range narrows considerably when we depart from assuming that the vote share depends *only* on the growth rate.)

In addition to taking into account the size of the standard error of the line when thinking about a prediction, we must also be cautious about the possible pitfalls from Lesson 5. If any of the pitfalls are relevant, we will at a minimum be using a standard error that is too small.

Prediction can help us see if the data mining problem is serious, at least if we are willing to wait for another observation. Say that by trying many variables we have found a variable that fits the 24 elections very well. If the truth is that this variable has no effect on the vote share, then the line that we have chosen is not likely to predict the next election well. We have searched using the 24 elections to find a line that looks good, but it is in fact spurious. Because the line is spurious, there is no reason to think it will do well for the next election, since the next election's outcome has not been used in the search. Observing how well a line predicts outside the period of the fit is thus a way of checking for possible data mining problems.

We have one more very important point to make about prediction. Remember that all we need to make a prediction of the vote share is a value for the growth rate. We used values of 3.0 and –3.0 earlier, but we could easily use other values. Once the actual growth rate for 2012 is known, we can also use it. The important point is that in terms of testing the theory, the actual growth rate should be used, not just some prediction of the growth rate. We want to compare the actual vote share for

2012 with the predicted vote share using the actual growth rate for 2012. Using any other growth rate would not be a test of the theory because the test would be based on an incorrect growth rate.

Finally, note that a prediction can be made for any observation in the sample period. That is, a prediction can be made for any of the 24 elections in Table 1-1 once the slope and intercept are estimated. This can be done because we know the actual value of the growth rate for each election. We just take the intercept, which is 50.9 from Box 2-1, and add to it 0.9 times the actual growth rate, where 0.9 is the estimated slope in Box 2-1. We in fact did this earlier when discussing the 1992 election. The predicted value for President Bush in 1992 is 50.9 plus 0.9 times 2.9, which is 53.5, where 2.9 is the actual value of the growth rate. The actual value of the vote share is 46.4 percent, and so the error is 7.1 percent. We can thus say that an error for any observation is simply the difference between the predicted value and the actual value.

Adding More Variables

The lessons in this chapter have been presented under the assumption that there is just one explanatory variable—the growth rate. We now must relax this assumption and consider more than one explanatory variable. In practice, there is almost always more than one explanatory variable. The theory of voting behavior outlined in Chapter 1, for example, is not that the vote share depends *only* on the growth rate. Other variables that were put forward are inflation, the number of good news quarters, whether the president is running for reelection, and a measure of duration. Fortunately, it is fairly easy to extend the analysis in this chapter to more than one explanatory variable. As an example, let's assume that the vote share depends on both the growth rate and inflation, as shown in Box 2-2.

BOX **2-2**

vote share depends on:	
	growth rate
	inflation
	intercept

When there is more than one variable, we can no longer use a graph like Figure 2-1 to help see what is going on. The line in Figure 2-1 is determined by two numbers, the intercept and the slope, but now we have three numbers to determine. From now on, we will use the word *coefficient* instead of slope to refer to the size of the effect associated with a variable. Using this terminology, the three numbers we have to determine in the present example are (1) the intercept, (2) the coefficient for the growth rate, and (3) the coefficient for inflation. Keep in mind that a coefficient is just a number, like 0.9.

The line that fits the points best in Figure 2-1 is the one that has the smallest sum of squared errors. We imagined a computer trying thousands of lines, computing the sum of squared errors for each line, and choosing the line with the smallest sum. Each line is characterized by a value for the intercept and a value for the slope (that is, a value for the coefficient for the growth rate).

For the present example, imagine the computer choosing three numbers: the intercept, the coefficient for the growth rate, and the coefficient for inflation. Given these three numbers, the computer can compute the error for each of the 24 elections. Consider, for example, the 1916 election, and assume that the three numbers are 51.0, 1.0, and –1.0. From Table 1-1 in Chapter 1, we see that the actual vote share for 1916 is 51.7, the growth rate is 2.2, and inflation is 4.3. Using the three numbers we have chosen, the predicted vote share for 1916 is 51.0 plus 1.0 times the growth rate of 2.2 and –1.0 times inflation of 4.3. The predicted vote share is thus 51.0 plus 2.2 minus 4.3 equal 48.9. The error for 1916 is then the predicted value of 48.9 minus the actual value of 51.7, or –2.8. Using the same three numbers, the computer can compute the errors for the other 23 elections in the same manner. Each error is the difference between the predicted value for that election and the actual value. These predictions are based on using the actual values of the growth rate and inflation. Once the 24 errors are computed, they can be squared and then summed.

We have so far seen that we can go from three numbers—the intercept, the coefficient for the growth rate, and the coefficient for inflation—to a value for the sum of squared errors. Now consider the computer doing this thousands of times, each time for a different set of three numbers, and in the end choosing the set of three numbers that has the smallest sum of squared errors associated with it. This best fitting set of three numbers is the analog of the best fitting line when there is only one explanatory variable.

Once the best fitting set of coefficients is found, we can compute the standard error. We first divide the sum of squared errors, which for our example turns out to be 486.1, by the number of observations (24) less the number of coefficients (3), or 21. This gives 23.1. We then take the square root to get 4.8. The standard error (a measure of the size of a typical error) is thus 4.8.

The thought experiment in Lesson 4 to derive the standard error of the estimated slope can be modified to incorporate more than one explanatory variable. For each set of 24 drawn errors (that is, for each universe), a best fitting set of coefficients is computed. After, say, 1,000 sets have been computed, a figure like Figure 2-3 can be drawn for each coefficient in the set. The standard error for a coefficient can then be determined by sweeping out 34.1 percent of the area as shown in Figure 2-3. The t-statistic for a coefficient is the coefficient divided by its standard error.

The results for the current example are presented in Box 2-3. The coefficient for the growth rate is 0.9, with a t-statistic of 4.8. Since the t-statistic is greater than 2.0, it is unlikely that the true coefficient for the growth rate is zero. The growth rate is significant. The coefficient for inflation is 0.1, with a t-statistic of 0.2. The t-statistic is very small, and so inflation is not significant. Also, the coefficient is positive, contrary to what theory says. There is thus no support for the theory that inflation has a negative effect on vote share. We will return to this result in the next chapter, where we will see that inflation is in fact significant with a negative coefficient when other explanatory variables are added. The main point here is that it is possible to compute the coefficient and its associated t-statistic for each explanatory variable. There is nothing new in principle here from the case of just one explanatory variable.

BOX **2-3**

vote share depends on:		t-statistic
0.9	growth rate	4.8
0.1	inflation	0.2
50.6	intercept	30.1
standard error: 4.8		
number of observations: 24		

Adding a third variable is also straightforward. There are then four coefficients to be computed instead of three, but all else is the same. In practice, it is quite easy for a computer to find the set of coefficients that leads to the smallest sum of squared errors. There are faster ways than the search procedure just discussed, but the answer is the same either way.

As a final point, we will sometimes use the phrase *other things being equal* in this book. This means we are engaging in the thought process of changing one explanatory variable without changing any of the others. For example, we might want to think about what happens to the vote share if the growth rate changes but inflation does not. We might then say that if the growth rate changes by such and such, the vote share will change by such and such, other things being equal. Other things being equal would mean that inflation does not change, nor does anything else that might affect the vote share.

Testing for Other Variables

We saw in the last section that each explanatory variable has associated with it a *t*-statistic. If the *t*-statistic for a particular variable is greater than 2.0 or less than –2.0, it is unlikely that the coefficient for the variable is zero. If the coefficient for the variable is not zero, then the variable has an effect on whatever is being explained, such as the vote share. It is thus easy to test whether a variable is supported by the data by including it in the fitting process and seeing if its *t*-statistic is greater than 2.0 or less than –2.0. This is a way of testing whether variables belong in the explanation (that is, whether variables are significant).

To give an example, say we are interested in whether the size of the armed forces affects the vote share. It may be that both the growth rate and the size of the armed forces affect the vote share. We can test for this by simply including the size of the armed forces along with the growth rate in the fitting process and seeing what the size of the *t*-statistic for the armed forces variable is.

Let's return now to possible pitfalls. Since it is so easy to try different variables or different sets of variables to see if they have large *t*-statistics, you can see why possible data mining is such a concern. Trying 100 combinations of variables and choosing the combination that leads to the best fit increases the chance that the chosen combination is spurious (that is, it is just a fluke). Again, theory needs to narrow the list of possible combinations.

We can now also be more precise about the problem of omitting the size of the armed forces from the explanation if it really belongs. If the growth rate tends to be high when the size of the armed forces is high and low when the size of the armed forces is low, and if both variables affect the vote share, then omitting the size of the armed forces will lead to a coefficient for the growth rate that is too large. For example, the 0.9 coefficient for the growth rate in Box 2-3 would be picking up the true effect of the growth rate on the vote share, which might be 0.6, and part of the effect of the size of the armed forces on the vote share, which might be 0.3. This would be an example of omitted variable bias, as mentioned in Lesson 5.

It is important to be clear on when there might be omitted variable bias. If an explanatory variable is omitted that truly affects the dependent variable, there will be no bias for the included explanatory variables if the omitted variable is uncorrelated with the included variables. The fit will not be as good because an explanatory variable has been omitted, but this will not bias the estimated effects of the other variables if they are not correlated with the omitted variable. The included variables will not be picking up any of the effect of the omitted variable because there is no correlation. The omitted variable needs to be correlated with the included explanatory variables for there to be omitted variable bias.

Horse Races

Many times in social science research we have two or more competing explanatory variables. For example, perhaps it is not the growth rate that affects the vote share but instead the change in the unemployment rate. These two variables are highly correlated because when the growth rate is high, the unemployment rate tends to decrease and vice versa. The two variables are not, however, perfectly correlated, and either variable is a plausible candidate for affecting votes for president.

Fortunately, it is easy to test between the growth rate and the change in the unemployment rate. We simply include both variables in the fitting process and compute the t-statistic for each. If one is significant (t-statistic larger than 2.0 or smaller than –2.0) and the other one is not, the one variable has dominated the other. We run, in other words, a *horse race* to see which variable dominates. We will perform a number of horse races in this book. A horse race is an effective way of allowing the data to choose which variable to keep. It is possible, of course, that both variables are significant or that neither variable is significant. In these two cases, the horse race is a dead heat (that is, the test is inconclusive).

Sensitivity or Robustness Checks

Related to horse races is the procedure of adding variables that you think from theory should not matter and thus should not be significant. If such variables are in fact significant, there is a possible problem with your theory. It is even a more serious problem if such variables are significant and adding them results in large changes in the other coefficients. In these cases, the results are said to be *sensitive* or to lack *robustness*. Adding variables that you think are unimportant is thus a way of looking for pitfalls. If the results are sensitive to such additions, this is a pitfall to worry about.

Another sensitivity check on possible data mining problems is the following. Say that we have found that the growth rate in the three-quarter period before an election is a significant explanatory variable in explaining the vote share in that election. This could be a fluke in the sense that we may have tried many variables before arriving at this one, and just by chance this one turned out to be significant. If the result is truly a fluke, then replacing the three-quarter growth rate with, say, the two-quarter growth rate or four-quarter growth rate should give very different results. On the other hand, if the growth rate does in fact affect the vote share, we would expect similar results using slightly different measures of the growth rate. For example, the two-quarter growth rate should give results similar to those using the three-quarter growth rate. Some sensitivity work is thus to replace certain explanatory variables with others that are similar to see how the results change. If the changes are large, this may be a cause for concern. We would like our results to be robust to small changes in the explanatory variables. More generally, we would like our results to be robust to small changes in the assumptions behind our theory and to small changes in the choice of data used.

Conclusion

We have covered a lot of material in this chapter, and if you have not seen any of it before, everything may not have completely sunk in. A good way to get an understanding of the tools is to see them in use, which is what the rest of this book is about. In the next chapter, we test the theory of voting behavior outlined in Chapter 1. In the present chapter, we simplified the theory to help in understanding the tools, but from now on, we will cut no corners.

As we go through each chapter, keep in mind the seven lessons: proposing a theory, collecting data, fitting the data, using the data to test the theory, thinking about pitfalls, examining the results, and making a prediction.

3   Presidential Elections

How can I, that girl standing there,
My attention fix
On Roman or on Russian
Or on Spanish politics?
Yet here's a travelled man that knows
What he talks about,
And there's a politician
That has read and thought,
And maybe what they say is true
Of war and war's alarms,
But O that I were young again
And held her in my arms!

William Butler Yeats, Politics

A Theory of Voting Behavior

The theory of voting behavior that we are going to test is discussed in Chapter 1. We summarized the theory in Box 1-1, which is repeated here as Box 3-1. The dependent variable is the vote share, and the explanatory variables are the other five variables in the box.

BOX **3-1**

vote share depends on:	
	growth rate
	inflation
	good news quarters
	president running
	duration

In Chapters 1 and 2, we have defined the vote share to be the incumbent party's share of the two-party vote (Democratic plus Republican). In this chapter, we will instead define the vote share to be the *Democratic* share of the two-party vote. This requires changing the sign of the economic variables when the incumbent party is Republican. If, for example, there is a large growth rate and the Republicans are in power, this has a positive effect on the Republican vote share and so a negative effect on the Democratic vote share. Therefore, if the Democratic share of the two-party vote is the dependent variable, the growth rate variable when the incumbent party is Republican should be the negative of the actual growth rate. A 4 percent growth rate would be –4 percent. We will continue to call the explanatory variables the growth rate, inflation, and good news quarters, but remember that the variables are the negative of the actual values when the incumbent party is Republican. This change makes no difference to the theory and results. For example, the coefficients of the economic variables corresponding to the best fit are the same, as are their *t*-statistics. The standard error is also the same. It is just sometimes easier to talk about the Democratic share across all elections than the incumbent-party share, so we will use the Democratic share.

We have discussed the theory in Chapter 1, and so we can move immediately to the data.

The Data

We are going to use the presidential elections from 1916 to 2008 to test the theory. The relevant data are listed in Table 1-1. Since any test of a theory is no better than the data behind it, we need to be clear regarding the exact variables that were used. We will discuss each of the variables in turn. Refer back to Table 1-1 as the various variables are discussed.

As mentioned in the previous section, the vote share that is used is the Democratic share of the two-party vote. For reference purposes, Table 1-1 lists both the incumbent-party share of the two-party vote and the Democratic share of the two-party vote. When the Democratic Party is the incumbent, the two shares are the same; otherwise the incumbent-party share is 100 minus the Democratic-Party share. The vote share is the two-party share, not the share of the total vote. Which vote share should be used depends on who the third-party voters are. To take an example, assume that before a third-party candidate came along, 30 percent of the voters were staunch Republicans, 30 percent were staunch

Democrats, and 40 percent were swing voters who were influenced by the economy. Assume also that the economy was neutral in the sense that half the swing voters were for the Democratic Party and half were for the Republican Party. In this case, the vote share for the Democratic Party would be 50 percent. This is, of course, both the total vote share and the two-party vote share, since there is no third party.

Now assume that a third-party candidate comes along and takes half of the swing voters who would have voted Republican and half who would have voted Democratic. In this case, both major parties get 40 percent of the total vote, with the third party getting 20 percent. The two-party vote share for both major parties is still 50 percent. The third-party candidate has thus lowered the total vote share for the Democratic Party from 50 percent to 40 percent, but the two-party vote share remains the same at 50 percent. It is thus clear that a third-party candidate can affect the total vote share in a big way, but the effect on the two-party vote share may be modest, depending on how much the candidate takes from one party versus the other. By using the two-party vote share, we are in effect assuming that third-party candidates take about the same amount from each major party.

The one exception to the use of the two-party vote share is the election of 1924. There is some evidence that LaFollette (the third-party candidate, running for the Progressive Party) took more votes from Davis (the Democrat) than from Coolidge (the Republican). It has been estimated (see the notes to this chapter) that 76.5 percent of the votes for LaFollette would otherwise have gone for Davis, with the remaining 23.5 percent going for Coolidge. The vote share for the Democratic Party was thus taken to be the number of votes that Davis got plus 76.5 percent of the votes that LaFollette got divided by the total number of votes for all three.

The growth rate that is used is the growth rate in the first three quarters (nine months) of the election year. Also, it is the *per capita* growth rate of real GDP, the growth rate of output per person. If the economy is growing only at the rate that population is growing, this is obviously less beneficial to the average person than if output per person is growing.

The measure of inflation is the average inflation rate over the 15 quarters prior to the election (that is, all the quarters of the administration except the last one). The variable used for inflation is the percentage change in the GDP deflator. As noted in Chapter 1, inflation and deflation are treated symmetrically: deflation is assumed to be just as bad in voters' minds as inflation.

The good news quarters variable is the number of quarters out of the 15 quarters before the election in which the growth rate exceeded 3.2 percent. (Remember, this is the per capita growth rate.) These are quarters in which the economy did exceptionally well, and the theory is that voters remember these kinds of events.

If the president is running for reelection, the president running variable is given a value of 1; otherwise, the value is 0. Vice presidents who became president during the administration were given a 1 if they ran again, except for Ford. Ford was given a 0 because he was not on the elected ticket but was appointed vice president when Agnew resigned. As with the economic variables, the president running variable is taken to be the negative of the value if the incumbent party is Republican.

The duration variable, which is listed in Table 1-1, is given a value of 0.0 if the incumbent party has only been in office for one consecutive term, 1.0 for two consecutive terms, 1.25 for three consecutive terms, 1.5 for four consecutive terms, and 1.75 for five consecutive terms. The duration variable is taken to be the negative of the value if the incumbent party is Republican.

This completes the discussion of the variables in Box 3-1, but there are two other variables that need to be mentioned. First, a party variable was included that has a value of 1 if the incumbent party is Democratic and −1 if the incumbent party is Republican. This variable is listed in Table 1-1. It tests whether there is a pure party effect. Second, the elections of 1920, 1944, and 1948 were treated somewhat differently because of the wars. The period prior to the 1920 election was dominated by World War I, and the periods prior to the 1944 and 1948 elections were dominated by World War II. The inflation variable and the good news quarters variable were assumed not to be relevant for these three elections. In other words, voters were assumed not to take into account past inflation and good news quarters when deciding how to vote during the three war-dominated periods. This treatment requires that a war variable be included that has a value of 1 for the 1920, 1944, and 1948 elections and a value of 0 otherwise. It also means that the values used for inflation and good news quarters for these three elections are 0, not the values listed in Table 1-1.

Fit and Test and Examine

We are now ready to see how well the explanatory variables do in explaining the vote share. Their coefficients are determined in the manner discussed in the last chapter. The set of coefficients is found that results in the smallest sum of squared errors, and the t-statistics are computed. The data used are from Table 1-1, with negative values used for the three economic variables, the president running variable, and the duration variable when the incumbent party is Republican. The results are shown in Box 3-2. In this case, there were eight coefficients to determine, one for each of the eight variables in the box (counting the intercept). There are thus eight corresponding t-statistics.

BOX **3-2**

vote share depends on:		t-statistic
0.67	growth rate	6.22
−0.65	inflation	−2.31
0.99	good news quarters	4.31
2.9	president running	2.18
−3.4	duration	−2.87
−1.9	party variable	−0.84
5.1	war variable	1.99
47.4	intercept	77.56
standard error: 2.5		
number of observations: 24		

It will be convenient after considering how well we have fit the data to discuss the size of the coefficients at the same time as we discuss their t-statistics. If we were exactly following the lessons in Chapter 2, we would not discuss the size of the coefficients until Saturday, after we had discussed the t-statistics and thought about possible pitfalls. Only if the t-statistics look good and the possible pitfalls seem minor should we care about the coefficients. We will be jumping ahead only for convenience of discussion.

Let's begin with the standard error in the box, which is 2.5. A typical error is thus 2.5, which is fairly small. As discussed in the last chapter,

TABLE **3-1**   Actual and predicted Democratic vote share

Year	Party in Power	Election Outcome	Actual Vote Share (%)	Predicted Vote Share (%)	Predicted Minus Actual (%)
1916	D	President Wilson beat Hughes	51.7	50.1	−1.6
1920	D	Cox lost to Harding	36.1	39.4	3.3
1924	R	President Coolidge beat Davis and LaFollette	41.7	42.4	0.7
1928	R	Hoover beat Smith	41.2	42.8	1.5
1932	R	President Hoover lost to F. Roosevelt	59.1	61.2	2.0
1936	D	President F. Roosevelt beat Landon	62.2	63.6	1.4
1940	D	President F. Roosevelt beat Willkie	55.0	55.5	0.5
1944	D	President F. Roosevelt beat Dewey	53.8	52.0	−1.7
1948	D	President Truman beat Dewey	52.3	50.8	−1.5
1952	D	Stevenson lost to Eisenhower	44.7	45.4	0.7
1956	R	President Eisenhower beat Stevenson	42.9	43.6	0.7
1960	R	Nixon lost to Kennedy	50.1	48.7	−1.4
1964	D	President Johnson beat Goldwater	61.2	60.9	−0.3
1968	D	Humphrey lost to Nixon	49.4	50.3	0.9
1972	R	President Nixon beat McGovern	38.2	41.5	3.3
1976	R	Ford lost to Carter	51.0	50.2	−0.9
1980	D	President Carter lost to Reagan	44.8	45.7	0.9
1984	R	President Reagan beat Mondale	40.9	38.2	−2.6
1988	R	G. Bush beat Dukakis	46.2	49.2	3.0
1992	R	President G. Bush lost to Clinton	53.6	48.8	−4.8
1996	D	President Clinton beat Dole	54.7	53.2	−1.5
2000	D	Gore lost to G. W. Bush	50.3	49.3	−1.0
2004	R	President G. W. Bush beat Kerry	48.8	45.5	−3.3
2008	R	McCain lost to Obama	53.7	55.2	1.5

we know that 68.2 percent of the time the error in predicting the vote share will be between −2.5 and 2.5.

We can get a more detailed picture of the errors by looking at Table 3-1. The table shows, for each of the 24 elections, the actual vote share, the predicted vote share, and the error (predicted minus actual). These predictions are based on the actual values of the explanatory variables. For each election, each coefficient in Box 3-2 was multiplied by the actual value of the respective variable for that coefficient, with the answers then added to get the predicted value for that election. If this is not completely clear, we will go over this procedure in more detail later in this chapter when we make a prediction for the 2012 election. You may also want to review the discussion of predictions at the end of Lesson 7 in Chapter 2.

The largest error in absolute value in Table 3-1 is for the 1992 election, when President George Bush got 48.8 percent of the vote and was predicted to get 53.6 percent, an error of –4.8 percentage points. The next three largest errors in absolute value are for the elections of 1920, 1972, and 2004. In 1920, Cox was predicted to get 39.4 percent and got 36.1 percent, an error of 3.3 percentage points. In 1972, Mc-Govern was predicted to get 41.5 percent and got 38.2 percent, also an error of 3.3 percentage points. And in 2004, Kerry was predicted to get 45.5 percent and got 48.8 percent, an error of –3.3 percentage points. All but 3 of the remaining 20 errors are less than 2 percentage points in absolute value.

Not counting 2000, three elections were predicted incorrectly as to the winner: 1960, 1968, and 1992. In 1960, Kennedy got 50.1 percent of the vote, a win, but was predicted to get 48.7 percent, an error of –1.4. In 1968, Humphrey got 49.4 percent of the vote, a loss, but was predicted to get 50.3 percent, an error of 0.9. Even though the winner was predicted incorrectly in these two elections, the errors are small, so in this sense the elections were predicted well. The 1992 error, on the other hand, was large, and the winner was also predicted incorrectly. For the 2000 election, Gore got 50.3 percent of the vote and was predicted to get 49.3 percent, an error of –1.0. In this case, the vote-share prediction was on the wrong side of 50 percent, predicting a Gore loss regarding the two-party vote share. In fact, Gore won the two-party vote share but lost the election in the electoral college.

Figure 3-1 plots the last column of Table 3-1. The errors are plotted for each election starting from the earliest. The large positive error for 1992 stands out in the figure.

Having examined the errors, let's now turn to the coefficients and their associated t-statistics. The coefficient for the growth rate is 0.67, which says that if the growth rate increases by 1.0, the vote share is predicted to increase by 0.67. The coefficient for inflation is –0.65, which says that if inflation increases by 1.0, the vote share is predicted to decrease by 0.65. The growth rate and inflation thus have similar effects on

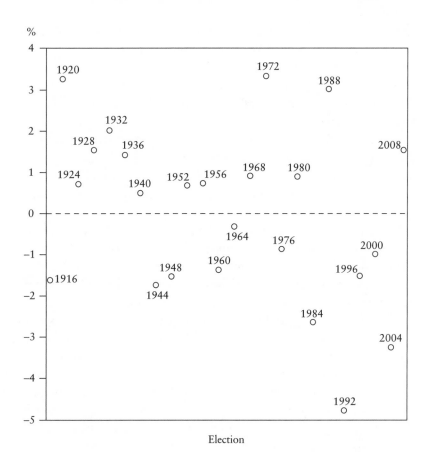

FIGURE **3-1**   Predicted minus actual vote share

the vote share except that one effect is positive and the other is negative. The t-statistic for the growth rate is 6.22, and since this value is considerably greater than 2.0, it is highly unlikely that the true coefficient for the growth rate is zero. In other words, it is quite likely that the growth rate affects the vote share. The t-statistic for inflation is –2.31, and since this value is less than –2.0, it is unlikely that the coefficient for inflation is zero. In other words, it is likely that inflation affects the vote share. The growth rate and inflation are thus both significant.

The significance of inflation in Box 3-2 is contrary to the results in Box 2-3, where inflation is not significant. This is an example of omitted variable bias. Box 2-3 has omitted a number of significant explanatory variables, namely, the additional variables in Box 3-2, and these omitted variables are correlated with inflation in such a way as to lead the coefficient on inflation in Box 2-3 to be too small in absolute value. Once the variables are added, the inflation coefficient increases in size in absolute value and becomes significant.

The coefficient for good news quarters is 0.99, which means that each additional good news quarter is predicted to increase the vote share by 0.99. This is a fairly large effect. The t-statistic for good news quarters is 4.31, so it is also unlikely that the true coefficient for good news quarters is zero.

The coefficient for the president running variable is 2.9, which means that a president running for another term is predicted to have a head start of 2.9 percentage points. The t-statistic is 2.18, so it is unlikely that the true coefficient is zero. If the true coefficient were zero, the president running would have no head start.

The duration variable has a coefficient of −3.4 with a t-statistic of −2.87. If a party has been in power for two consecutive terms, it is predicted to start out behind by 3.4 percentage points because the duration variable has a value of 1.0 in this case. If a party has been in power for three consecutive terms, it is predicted to start out behind by 3.4 times 1.25, or 4.25 percentage points, because the duration variable has a value of 1.25 in this case. For four consecutive terms, the value is 3.4 times 1.50, or 5.1 percentage points, and so on. The duration variable is significant because its t-statistic is less than −2.0.

The coefficient for the party variable is −1.9 with a t-statistic of −0.84. Remember that the party variable has a value of 1 if the Democratic Party is the incumbent party and −1 if the Republican Party is the incumbent party. The variable is not significant because the t-statistic is less than 2.0 in absolute value. It could be deleted without changing the results much. If it is retained, the coefficient of −1.9 means the following. Say that all the other variables have a value of zero. Then if the incumbent party is Democratic, the predicted Democratic vote share is the intercept, 47.4, minus 1.9, or 45.5. If the incumbent party is Republican, the predicted Democratic vote share is the intercept, 47.4, plus 1.9, or 49.3. The predicted Republican vote share is 100 minus the predicted Democratic vote share, or 50.7 when the Republican Party is the incumbent party.

Therefore, other things being equal, the Republican Party starts off when it is the incumbent party with a predicted vote share that is larger than the predicted vote share for the Democratic Party when it is the incumbent party (50.7 versus 45.5). If the party variable is dropped and the coefficients are reestimated, the intercept is 47.5. This implies that if all the other variables have a value of zero, the Democratic Party starts off when it is the incumbent party with a predicted vote share of 47.5 and the Republican Party starts off when it is the incumbent party with a predicted vote share of 100 minus this, or 52.5. Either with or without the party variable included, the results show a bias in favor of the Republicans, other things being equal.

The coefficient for the war variable is only relevant for three elections. Its t-statistic is 1.99. The war variable is thus significant if we use a cutoff of 2.0 and round 1.99 up to 2.0.

Overall, the results seem very good. The errors are small except for 1992, and all the variables are significant except for the party variable. In particular, the t-statistics for the economic variables (the growth rate, inflation, and good news quarters) suggest that the economy does have an effect on the vote share; it is very unlikely that we would get these t-statistics if the economy did not affect the vote share. We cannot, however, relax because of the possible pitfalls lurking in the background. To these we now turn.

Possible Pitfalls

The main pitfall that we need to worry about is the possibility of data mining. Many variables were tried in arriving at the final results, and we have only 24 observations. It may be that by chance we have fit the data well, but in fact, the vote share is determined by other things. The following are the main things that were tried that may be subject to the data mining problem.

- Increments other than 0.25 were tried for the duration variable, and 0.25 was chosen because it gave the best results in terms of fit.
- Values other than 3.2 percent were tried for the cutoff for good news quarters, and 3.2 was chosen because it gave the best results in terms of fit.

- The particular treatment for the wars for the three elections was done because this led to an improved fit.
- Different periods for the growth rate were tried, and the particular one chosen, the first three quarters of the election year, gave the best results in terms of fit.
- Different periods for inflation were also tried, and the particular one chosen, the entire four-year period except for the last quarter, gave the best results in terms of fit.
- After the large error was made in 1992, an attempt was made to find reasons for it. This effort led to the choice of the good news quarters variable, which prior to 1992 had not been thought of. The good news quarters variable helps make the error for 1992 smaller because, as you can see from Table 1-1, there were only two good news quarters for the George Bush administration. President Bush is still predicted to win in 1992 in Table 3-1, but by less than he would be predicted to if it were not for the good news quarters variable.

With only 24 elections and all this searching, it is certainly possible that the results in Box 3-2 are a fluke and are not really right. As discussed in Chapter 2, one way of examining the seriousness of the data mining problem is to see how well future observations are predicted. If the results are a fluke, future predictions should not in general be very accurate. In particular, if the results are a fluke, the prediction for the 2012 election is not likely to be accurate, since no information about this election was used in getting the results. The prediction of the 2012 election is discussed later in this chapter.

An alternative approach to examining the data mining problem is to use only part of the observations to get the coefficients and then see how well these coefficients do in predicting the other observations. This is not as good a check as waiting because we have used information in the whole sample (both parts) to decide which variables to include, but at least the coefficients are obtained using only the information in the first part of the observations.

To perform this check, the best fitting set of coefficients was obtained using only the elections through 1960. In other words, the best fit was obtained for the 1916–1960 period (12 elections), and no data from

1964 or later were used. The best fitting coefficients for this set of observations are shown in Box 3-3. These coefficients obviously differ from the
earlier ones because they are based on only 12 observations rather than
24. The coefficient for the growth rate still has a large t-statistic, and its
value has changed only slightly—from 0.67 to 0.80. The t-statistic for the
inflation coefficient, however, is now only –1.15. The inflation coefficient
has changed from –0.65 to –0.42. The results are thus weak for inflation
affecting the vote share if the observations used stop in 1960.

BOX **3-3**

Estimation period 1916–1960		
vote share depends on:		t-statistic
0.80	growth rate	7.78
−0.42	inflation	−1.15
0.72	good news quarters	2.99
5.0	president running	3.99
−2.2	duration	−2.42
−2.9	party variable	−1.35
4.3	war variable	1.85
46.4	intercept	79.58
standard error: 1.5		
number of observations: 12		

Perhaps the most important result is that the t-statistic for good
news quarters is still fairly large (2.99). Even though the good news quarters variable was not formulated until after the 1992 election, its significance does not depend on the 1992 observation. Even stopping in 1960,
the results say that a zero coefficient for goods news quarters is unlikely.
The size of the coefficient has fallen from 0.99 to 0.72, although it is still
significant.

We can use this new set of coefficients to predict the outcomes of
the elections after 1960. These predictions are presented in Table 3-2.
They are based on using the actual values of the explanatory variables,
as are those in Table 3-1. The predictions in the two tables differ because
they are based on the use of different coefficients. If data mining is a

TABLE **3-2**   Actual and predicted Democratic vote share: 1960 coefficients

Year	Party in Power	Election Outcome	Actual Vote Share (%)	Predicted Vote Share (%)	Predicted Minus Actual (%)
1964	D	President Johnson beat Goldwater	61.2	59.2	−2.0
1968	D	Humphrey lost to Nixon	49.4	49.1	−0.3
1972	R	President Nixon beat McGovern	38.2	38.7	0.5
1976	R	Ford lost to Carter	51.0	48.0	−3.0
1980	D	President Carter lost to Reagan	44.8	45.9	1.0
1984	R	President Reagan beat Mondale	40.9	36.4	−4.5
1988	R	G. Bush beat Dukakis	46.2	48.1	1.9
1992	R	President G. Bush lost to Clinton	53.6	44.6	−9.0
1996	D	President Clinton beat Dole	54.7	53.1	−1.6
2000	D	Gore lost to G. W. Bush	50.3	47.3	−3.0
2004	R	President G. W. Bush beat Kerry	48.8	43.0	−5.8
2008	R	McCain lost to Obama	53.7	53.9	0.2

serious problem, the predictions in Table 3-2 should not in general be very good because the coefficients have been estimated using only data through 1960.

The predictions in Table 3-2 are in fact fairly good. The largest error is for 1992, where it is –9.0. The next largest error is for 2004, when Kerry got 48.8 percent of the vote and was predicted to get only 43.0 percent, an error of –5.8. The error for 1984 is –4.5 percent, and otherwise, the errors are less than or equal to 3 percentage points in absolute value. Remember that by the 2008 election, the prediction was based on a set of coefficients that was chosen using data ending 48 years earlier!

Sensitivity checks to small changes in some of the assumptions have also been made. The coefficients are fairly robust to (1) the use of 2.7 or 3.7 percent instead of 3.2 percent as the cutoff for good news quarters, (2) the use of 0.00 or 0.50 instead of 0.25 as the increment for the duration variable, and (3) counting Ford as an incumbent running again for the president running variable. The results are more sensitive to the treatment of the two world wars. If the adjustment for the wars is not made, the t-statistic for inflation falls in absolute value to –1.67, although both the growth rate and good news quarters remain significant with only slightly smaller coefficients. The fits are worse if the growth rate is only for the second and third quarters of the election year or for the four quarters before the election, but the growth rate always remains highly significant. The inflation variable loses its significance if only 11 quarters or only 7 quarters before the election are used instead of 15, although its coefficient is always negative. The results are thus fairly robust to small changes in some of the assumptions.

The analysis in this section thus suggests that data mining may not be a serious problem, but one can never be sure. The results need to be interpreted with some caution. This is particularly true in light of the large error for 1992. Perhaps 1992 is just an unusual draw—something unlikely to happen very often—but it could also signal something more serious. It is encouraging, however, that for the four elections since 1992, the errors are modest in Table 3-1.

What About the Electoral College?

Nothing has been said so far about the electoral college. The dependent variable (that is, the variable to be explained) has been taken to be the Democratic share of the two-party vote, not the Democratic share in the electoral college. A candidate can get more than 50 percent of the two-party vote and yet lose the election in the electoral college, as happened to Gore in 2000. This also happened in 1876 (Hayes versus Tilden) and in 1888 (Harrison versus Cleveland).

The aim of our analysis is to explain voting behavior in the sense of explaining how many votes one party gets relative to the other in the whole country. The aim is not to explain how many states go for one party over the other.

Nor is the aim of the analysis to explain who wins the election. The theory is judged by how close the predicted values of the two-party vote share are to the actual values (that is, by the size of the errors). Consider two hypothetical elections in which the incumbent party is the Democratic Party and in which it wins both times. Say the party's vote share is 61 percent in the first election and 51 percent in the second. Say also that the predicted vote share is 54 percent for the first election and 49 percent for the second. The winner was thus correctly predicted for the first election, but the error was fairly large at −7 percentage points; much of the large margin for the Democrats was not predicted. On the other hand, the winner was incorrectly predicted for the second election, but the error was small at 2 percentage points. The election was predicted to be close and it was. The second election is thus predicted better than the first even though the winner was predicted incorrectly in the second. As a social scientist trying to explain the vote share, I care about the size of my errors, not about who wins. This point is not always easy to get across to reporters, and I sometimes sound uncaring.

Do Campaigns Matter?

Nothing has been said about campaigns. Does this mean that campaigns don't matter, and all that matters are the incumbency information and the economic variables? What if one party campaigned and the other did not? Wouldn't this make a difference? This is a commonly asked question, especially by those considering working on a campaign. A related question that is sometimes asked is whether it matters who is nominated. What if some extreme left- or right-wing candidate were nominated? Wouldn't this have a big effect on the outcome?

The answer is that campaigns are likely to matter and that the nomination of an extreme candidate is likely to make a difference. This does not, however, call into question the above analysis, and the reason is somewhat subtle to grasp. Remember what is being explained—the voting that actually takes place on Election Day. It seems safe to say that in all 24 elections, both parties campaigned hard. Each party did its best, given the issues and so forth. Each of the 24 vote shares is thus based on strong campaigns by both parties. In none of the 24 elections did one party not campaign, so our analysis has nothing to say about what would happen if one party did not campaign. We are asking the question of what determines the vote share *given* that both parties campaign hard (which they always do).

Similarly, extremists are not nominated by the two parties (yes, I know, some will disagree with this statement), so our analysis has nothing to say about what would happen if a party nominated one. Again, we are asking the question of what determines the vote share *given* that both parties nominate nonextremists.

To take one more example, say that two months before an election, some new campaign tactic of one of the parties, such as negative ads, appears to be working well. The other party is likely to counter with its own negative ads, and in the end, the new tactics of the two parties would probably roughly cancel each other out. Again, each party has done its best by election time, and we are looking at voting behavior after all the hard campaigning has been done.

Manipulating the Economy to Increase Votes

As previously discussed, different periods for the growth rate were tried, and the period that led to the best results in terms of fit was the first three quarters of the election year. The growth rates in the other quarters matter in that they can contribute to the number of good news quarters, but they do not get extra weight beyond this. Voters appear to give the more recent experience more weight—"recent" in this case being the election year. This weighting is consistent with a number of psychological experiments, where what happens at the end of an experiment is remembered more than what happens otherwise (see the Notes to Chapter 1).

Because a strong growth rate in the year of the election is good for the incumbent party, there is an incentive for the incumbent party to try to stimulate the economy in the election year to help get reelected. One strategy would be to slow the economy in the beginning of the four-year term and then stimulate hard in the final year and a half or so. Slowing the economy in the beginning would allow more room for rapid growth rate at the end. If this were done, there would be a four-year business cycle in which the trough would be reached near the middle of the period and the peak would be reached near the end. This type of business cycle is called a *political business cycle*. The cycle is political in that it is induced by the incumbent party manipulating the economy for its own political purpose.

Whether this strategy has been pursued at some points in the past (that is, whether there are in fact political business cycles) is difficult to test. There are four-year periods in which a trough was reached in the middle and a peak at the end, but it is hard do know if this was done deliberately by the party in power. There is also the question of whether an administration has the ability to manipulate the economy in such a precise way, especially if the other party has control of Congress. Possibly, some have tried and failed. This question of how parties behave regarding the economy once in power is not the same as the question of how voters behave, and we have only been concerned in this chapter with the behavior of voters.

Does Congress Matter?

An implicit assumption behind our theory of voting behavior is that voters praise or blame the White House, not the Congress, for the state of the economy. If one party controls the White House and the other controls the Congress, who should be judged? The above theory is obviously wrong if the answer is Congress, and this is another possible pitfall that should be kept in mind. Casual observation suggests that the buck stops at the White House, but we have simply assumed this to be true and have not tested it.

Do Voters Really Know the Growth Rate and Inflation Numbers?

I have often been asked if I really believe that many voters know the actual values of the growth rate and inflation when they enter the voting booth on Election Day. How many people really look up the numbers in their newspapers before voting? (This is usually a hostile question.) It is surely unlikely that many voters know the exact numbers. They form their opinions about the economy by looking at the conditions around them—how their friends and neighbors and employers are doing—not by looking at the numbers themselves. They may also be influenced by the media, especially radio and television commentators. The numbers, however, are likely to be related to the conditions that people are observing. If the growth rate is negative, for example, it is likely that the conditions that people see around them are not so good and that commentators are saying bad things about the economy. It is thus not necessary that voters know the exact numbers as long as the numbers accurately reflect what the voters are actually paying attention to.

Real-Time Predictions of the Eight Elections Between 1980 and 2008

A prediction of a dependent variable, like the vote share, is based on a particular choice of explanatory variables—a particular box in a book if you will, a particular set of coefficients, and a particular set of values of the explanatory variables. A special case of a prediction, which we will call a *real-time prediction*, is one that was actually made before the event in question, like an election, took place. For example, I made a real-time prediction of the 2008 election on October 29, 2008, a few days before the actual election occurred. This prediction used the explanatory variables in Box 3-2, coefficients that were based on observations through the 2004 election, and values of the economic variables that were available at the time. This predicted value is not the same as the predicted value for 2008 in Table 3-1. The predicted value for 2008 in Table 3-1 is based on the same choice of explanatory variables, but the coefficients differ slightly because they are based on using one more observation—the 2008 observation that was not available until after the election. Also, the values of the economic variables used for the predictions in Table 3-1 are the latest revised values. They are not exactly the same as those that were available on October 29, 2008, because economic data get revised over time.

The voting analysis in this chapter was first developed in 1978. This allowed a real-time prediction to be made for 1980. Since that time, I have made real-time predictions for seven other elections, 1984 through 2008. In each case, I used the coefficients and economic data that were available before the election. As mentioned earlier in this chapter, the choice of explanatory variables was changed slightly following the 1992 election. In particular, the good news quarters variable was added. No changes in explanatory variables have been made since then. This means that the explanatory variables in Box 3-2 were slightly different for the elections before 1996. The eight real-time predictions are presented in Table 3-3 along with the actual values and the corresponding errors.

Also presented in Table 3-3 are the predictions in Table 3-1. These predictions use all the information through the 2008 election. The economic data are the latest revised data, and the coefficients are based on using observations through 2008. The explanatory variables are those in Box 3-2. These predictions obviously use more information than the real-time predictions, which only use the information available before the particular election predicted. Because of this, it seems likely that on average the real-time predictions will not be as accurate as the predictions in

TABLE **3-3**   Real-time and Table 3-1 predictions: Democratic share of the
two-party vote

Year	Actual	REAL-TIME		TABLE 3-1	
		Predicted	*Error*	*Predicted*	*Error*
1980	44.8	46.4	1.6	45.7	0.9
1984	40.9	43.2	2.3	38.2	−2.6
1988	46.2	48.1	1.9	49.2	3.0
1992	53.6	43.1	−10.5	48.8	−4.8
1996	54.7	51.0	−3.7	53.2	−1.5
2000	50.3	50.8	0.5	49.3	−1.0
2004	48.8	42.3	−6.5	45.5	−3.3
2008	53.7	51.9	−1.8	55.2	1.5
Average absolute error			3.60		2.33

Table 3-1. This is in fact the case. The average absolute error in Table 3-3 for the real-time predictions across the eight elections is 3.60 percentage points, which compares to 2.33 percentage points for the Table 3-1 predictions.

The largest errors in Table 3-3 are for the elections of 1992 and 2004. In 1992, Clinton, running against President George Bush, got 53.6 percent of the vote and was predicted to get much less—the real-time error is –10.5 percentage points. In 2004, Kerry, running against President George W. Bush, got 48.8 percent of the vote and was predicted to get much less—the real-time error is –6.5 percentage points. The other six elections are predicted fairly well. Excluding 2000, which is hard to know how to count regarding the winner because of the difference between the popular vote outcome and the electoral college outcome, only 1992 was forecast incorrectly as to the winner.

Although the choice of explanatory variables was changed slightly following the 1992 election, in part to try to improve the prediction of the 1992 election, this election remains a poorly predicted one. The error in Table 3-1 for 1992 is the largest of the 24 errors (ignoring sign) at –4.8 percentage points.

The main point of this section is to realize that the accuracy of real-time predictions is likely to be worse that the accuracy of predictions like those in Table 3-1, which are based on more information.

Predictions of the 2012 Election

If President Obama runs for reelection, we know the following before the election of 2012: the president running variable has a value of 1;
the duration variable has a value of 0.0; the party variable has a value of
1; and the war variable has a value of 0. However, we do not know the
values of the economic variables until a few days before the election. At
the time of this writing (November 2010), economic data are available
through the third quarter of 2010. There are eight more quarters before the election in November 2012. So far, we know that there has been
one good news quarter since the first quarter of 2009, and inflation has
been low at a rate of about 1 percent.

To predict the 2012 vote share, we need to choose values of the
growth rate in 2012, of inflation over the 15 quarters, and of the number
of good news quarters. So we need three numbers before we can predict
the vote share. Table 3-4 shows three predictions. The first is based on the
assumption of a robust recovery in 2011 and 2012, the second is based
on the assumption of a very modest recovery, and the third is based on
the assumption of a recession in 2012—a so-called double dip recession.

In the case of a strong recovery, the predicted vote share for President Obama is 55.9 percent. In this case, he is predicted to get a larger
vote share than he did in 2008, which was 53.7 percent. In the case of a
modest recovery, Obama is predicted to get 49.1 percent, which is a narrow loss. In the case of a double dip recession, he is predicted to get 46.4
percent, which is a fairly large loss.

Whether President Obama is predicted to win or lose thus comes
down to what the economy will be in the next two years. This is, of

TABLE **3-4**   Predictions for 2012 Democratic share of the two-party vote

	ECONOMIC VALUES			
Predicted share	Growth Rate	Inflation	Good News Quarters	
55.9	3.7	1.4	6	Robust economic recovery
49.1	1.0	1.4	1	Modest economic recovery
46.4	−3.0	1.4	1	Double dip recession

course, what the analysis in this chapter is all about—the economy matters. By the time you are reading this, you will know more about the economy in 2011 and 2012 than I know now. You can use the coefficients in Box 3-2 and your own assumptions about the growth rate, inflation, and the number of good new quarters to make your own prediction of the vote share. To make this clear, the following discussion spells out exactly what you need to do to make a prediction for 2012.

We begin with the coefficients in Box 3-2. To make a prediction for 2012, we multiply each coefficient by a chosen value of its corresponding variable, with the answers then being added to get the predicted value. Box 3-4 lists the calculations using the economic values corresponding to a strong recovery. These economic values are 3.7 percent for the growth rate, 1.4 percent for inflation, and 6 for the number of good news quarters. You can see that the sum of the individual multiplications is 55.9 percent—the predicted percentage for Obama.

BOX **3-4**

Real-time prediction for 2012			
coef.	value	coef. × value	
0.67	3.7	2.5	growth rate
−0.65	1.4	−0.9	inflation
0.99	6	5.9	good news quarters
2.9	1	2.9	president running
−3.4	0.0	0.0	duration
−1.9	1.0	−1.9	party variable
5.1	0.0	0.0	war variable
47.4	1.0	47.4	intercept
		55.9	TOTAL (vote share)

A calculator on my Web site does this work for you. If you give it your own values of the three economic variables, it will calculate the predicted vote share. It is simply doing what is done in Box 3-4 for your particular values of the growth rate, inflation, and the number of good news quarters.

You might ask how much confidence should you put on any particular prediction for 2012. The standard error in Box 3-2 is 2.5 percentage points; thus, from the analysis in Chapter 2, we should expect the prediction error to be between –2.5 and 2.5 about 68.2 percent of the time and to be between –5.0 and 5.0 a little over 95 percent of the time. The actual degree of uncertainty is, however, greater than this. First, there are the possible pitfalls, which could be important. Second, we know from Table 3-3 that real-time predictions are in general less accurate than predictions like those in Table 3-1. This was discussed earlier. (Any prediction before the 2012 election is obviously a real-time prediction.) The standard error of 2.5 is estimated using the errors in Table 3-1, and so it is too low when applied to real-time predictions. Third, any prediction that you make before all the economic data are in (which is not until right before the election) will be using economic values that are themselves subject to error.

If we look at the real-time predictions in Table 3-3 for the last four elections, the average error is 3.1 percentage points. These are the elections that were predicted after the changes that were made following the 1992 election. This suggests that you might think of the standard error as being about 3 percentage points rather than 2.5 percentage points for your real-time prediction for 2012. And then, added on to this degree of uncertainty should be the uncertainty that you attach to your choice of economic values.

Conclusion

This chapter is an example of the use of the tools in Chapter 2. A theory of voting behavior is proposed, data are collected, and the theory is tested. This example is interesting because there are many possible pitfalls to think about. It is also interesting in that once we get to prediction (on Sunday), an important event can be predicted—namely, the outcome of the 2012 presidential election. We now turn to Congress.

4 Congressional Elections

The proudest now is but my peer,
The highest not more high;
To-day, of all the weary year,
A king of men am I.
To-day, alike are great and small,
The nameless and the known;
My palace is the people's hall,
The ballot-box my throne!
Who serves to-day upon the list
Beside the served shall stand;
Alike the brown and wrinkled fist,
The gloved and dainty hand!
The rich is level with the poor,
The weak is strong to-day;
And sleekest broadcloth counts no more
Than homespun frock of gray.
To-day let pomp and vain pretence
My stubborn right abide;
I set a plain man's common sense
Against the pedant's pride.
To-day shall simple manhood try
The strength of gold and land;
The wide world has not wealth to buy
The power in my right hand!
While there's a grief to seek redress,
Or balance to adjust,
Where weighs our living manhood less
Than Mammon's vilest dust,
While there's a right to need my vote,
A wrong to sweep away,
Up! clouted knee and ragged coat!
A man's a man to-day!

John Greenleaf Whittier, The Poor Voter on Election Day

A Theory of Voting Behavior

We can use the theory of voting behavior in the last chapter to examine congressional elections. Is it the case that the economy also affects votes for Congress? We will see that the answer is yes. The variable we will examine is the Democratic share of the two-party vote for the House of Representatives. There are actually two variables to examine, the vote share for the House in the years there is also a presidential election, called the *on-term* House election, and the vote share for the House in the years there is only a congressional election, called the *midterm* House election.

The task in this chapter is straightforward. We want to see if the economic variables that we found in the last chapter are important in explaining the presidential vote share are also important in explaining the House vote share. We will continue to assume that voters praise or blame the party in power in the White House for the economy. We assume this to be true for the House vote even if the party that controls the House is not the party in power in the White House. The buck stops with the party in the White House.

The three economic variables used in the last chapter are the growth rate, inflation, and the number of good news quarters, and we continue to use these. We will also use the president running variable for the on-term House election, under the assumption that if the president is running again, he may be able to use his power to help congressional candidates. We also continue to use the party variable and the war variable.

Are there any other influences on votes for the House that we might try to account for? There are strong incumbency advantages for representatives. Once a congressman or congresswoman is in, he or she tends to stay in for a long time. The power of his or her office is strong at the individual level—think pork. Given this, if a party did well in the previous House election—receiving a large vote share and many seats—this may have a positive effect on how it does in the current election. The party would have many incumbents, which may help in the current election. So an additional variable that we will try is the House vote share in the previous House election—the midterm vote share for the next on-term election and the on-term vote share for the next midterm election.

There is much discussion in the political science literature on whether there is a presidential coattail effect on the on-term congressional elections. If the presidential candidate does well, does this positively affect votes for his party in Congress? It is the case that a party's vote share for president is highly correlated with its vote share for the House. But as we discussed in Chapter 2, correlation does not necessarily mean causation. If, for example, the economy affects both vote shares, the shares will be correlated, but the driving force is the economy, not one vote share directly affecting the other. We can in fact test whether there is a coattail effect, and it will show that this effect is not significant. The two vote shares tend to move together because they have common explanatory variables.

Another issue discussed in the political science literature is whether voters like *balance*. Do voters like to limit the control that any one party has over the country? This is hard to test because the concept of balance is murky, but we have found one interesting result regarding the midterm House vote. We will see that a party's vote share in a presidential election has a negative effect on the party's vote share in the next midterm House election. Why might this be the case? It can't be a reversal of a positive presidential coattail effect in the previous election because there is no evidence of any coattail effect in the first place. It also can't simply be a vote against the party in the White House at the time of the midterm election because it is the *size* of the previous presidential vote share that matters, not which party controls the White House. For example, if the Democrats get 52 percent in one presidential election and 58 percent in another, winning both times, the lagged presidential vote-share variable says that the Democrats will get a smaller midterm House vote share in the second case than in the first, other things being equal, even though they are in power in the White House in both cases. A possible explanation for the negative presidential effect is the balance argument. If voters, other things being equal, don't like one party becoming too dominant, they may tend to vote more against a party in the midterm election the better the party has done in the previous presidential election.

Another feature to consider about the midterm House vote is the timing issue. Only 7 quarters have elapsed at the time of the midterm election from the time the new (or reelected) president took power compared to 15 quarters for the on-term election. The economic variables for the midterm election must thus pertain to the first 7 quarters of the administration rather than the first 15.

There is one other issue we need to consider. In Box 3-2 for the presidential vote share, the growth rate coefficient is 0.67, the inflation coefficient is –0.65, and the good news quarters coefficient is 0.99. The growth rate and inflation coefficients are thus about equal in absolute value, and the good news quarters coefficient is about 50 percent greater. Possibly, the overall effect of the economy on the vote share is different for the presidential election than for the House elections, but yet the relative weights (0.67, –0.65, and 0.99) are the same. Consider the on-term House election. If the weights are the same, only one economic variable should be included as an explanatory variable. This variable, which will be called *index1*, is 0.67 times the growth rate minus 0.65 times inflation and plus 0.99 times good news quarters. The coefficient for index1 is the estimate of the overall effect of the economy on the on-term House vote share. If, for example, it is less than 1.0 but significant, this says that the economy affects the House vote share but less than it does the presidential vote share. The relative weights of the three economic variables are, however, the same. We can test whether the relative weights are the same, and we will discuss that later in this chapter. The results suggest that the weights are the same, and so we will use index1 in the following analysis.

For the midterm House election, the three economic variables are different, as has been noted. The growth rate that was tried is the growth rate in the three quarters before the midterm election, and it turned out not to be significant. The growth rates two quarters before the election and four quarters before the election were also not significant. The growth rate was thus not included among the economic explanatory variables for the midterm House election. The inflation variable tried is the inflation rate for the seven quarters before the election, and the good news quarters variable tried is the number of quarters out of the seven in which there was a large growth rate. Both of these variables are significant. In addition, the results suggest that the relative weights on the two variables from the presidential results, namely, –0.65 and 0.99, are the same after the good news quarters variable is multiplied by 15/7 to make it comparable in units to the good news quarters variable for the presidential election. We will thus include as the economic explanatory variable for the midterm House election a variable, called *index2*, which is –0.65 times inflation plus 0.99 times 15/7 times the number of good news quarters.

This theory is summarized in Boxes 4-1 and 4-2.

BOX **4-1**

House on-term vote share depends on:	
	index1
	president running
	party variable
	war variable
	House vote share lagged
	intercept
index1 is 0.66 times growth rate minus 0.65 times inflation plus 0.99 times good news quarters	

BOX **4-2**

House midterm vote share depends on:	
	index2
	party variable
	war variable
	House vote share lagged
	presidential vote share lagged
	intercept
index2 is −0.65 times inflation plus 0.99 times 15/7 times good news quarters	

The Data

The sample period for the on-term House election is the same as the sample period for the presidential election, 1916–2008, 24 elections. The economic explanatory variables are those in Table 1-1. The variable to be explained is the Democratic share of the two-party House vote in the on-term election. The two additional variables needed from those in Table 1-1 are the on-term and midterm House vote shares. The midterm House vote share is needed because it is an explanatory variable for the next on-term House election. Observations on the on-term House vote share are presented later in this chapter in Table 4-2 under the column Actual Vote Share. You can see in this table, for example, that in the last two on-term elections, the Democrats got 48.6 percent of the vote in 2004 and 55.5 percent in 2008. The midterm House vote share is discussed next.

The sample period for the midterm House election is from 1918 through 2010, also 24 elections. The variable to be explained is the Democratic share of the two-party House vote in the midterm election. In this case, the explanatory economic variables are different because the relevant period is only 7 quarters before the election rather than 15. The observations on the vote share and the economic variables are presented

TABLE **4-1**   Data used for explaining the midterm House vote share

Year	Democratic Vote Share (%)	Party in Power 1 = D −1 = R	War	Inflation Rate (%)	Good News Quarter
1914	50.3	—	—	—	—
1918	45.1	1	1	15.7	10.7
1922	46.4	−1	0	11.5	12.9
1926	41.6	−1	0	0.1	10.7
1930	45.7	−1	0	2.6	4.3
1934	56.5	1	0	4.1	8.6
1938	50.8	1	0	0.0	6.4
1942	47.7	1	1	8.0	15.0
1946	45.3	1	1	10.0	4.3
1950	50.0	1	0	0.1	6.4
1954	52.5	−1	0	0.8	2.1
1958	56.0	−1	0	2.7	2.1
1962	52.5	1	0	1.2	8.6
1966	51.2	1	0	2.6	10.7
1970	54.4	−1	0	5.0	2.1
1974	58.5	−1	0	8.2	4.3
1978	54.4	1	0	6.7	8.6
1982	56.0	−1	0	7.0	4.3
1986	55.1	−1	0	2.5	2.1
1990	54.2	−1	0	3.9	2.1
1994	46.5	1	0	2.2	4.3
1998	49.5	1	0	1.4	6.4
2002	47.6	−1	0	1.9	0.0
2006	54.1	−1	0	3.4	2.1
2010	45.9	1	0	1.0	2.1

NOTE: Observation of the midterm House vote share for 1914 needed for explaining the on-term House vote share.

in Table 4-1. The growth rate is not presented because, as noted in the last section, it was not significant and was dropped. You can see that in the last two midterm elections, the Democrats got 54.1 percent of the vote in 2006 and 45.9 percent in 2010.

Fit and Test and Examine

We will consider the on-term House vote first. The explanatory variables are listed in Box 4-1. The data used are from Tables 1-1 and 4-1. Remember that when the incumbent party is Republican, negative values are used for the three economic variables (and thus for index1) and the president running variable. The coefficients for the explanatory variables are determined in the manner discussed in Chapter 2. The set of coefficients is found that results in the smallest sum of squared errors, and the t-statistics are computed. The results are shown in Box 4-3.

BOX **4-3**

House on-term vote share depends on:		t-statistic
0.57	index1	6.65
2.5	president running	2.70
−3.9	party variable	−4.56
3.2	war variable	1.93
0.62	House vote share lagged − 50.0	5.54
49.6	intercept	93.00
standard error: 2.1		
number of observations: 24		
0.38	growth rate	
−0.37	inflation	
0.56	good news quarters	

The coefficient for index1 is 0.57 with a t-statistic of 6.65. The economic variables are thus significant. The coefficient is less than 1.0, which means that the economic variables have a smaller effect on the House vote share than they do on the presidential vote share. The effect is 57 percent of the size of the effect for the presidential vote share. The implied coefficients for the economic variables are presented at the bottom of Box 4-3. The weights are 0.67, –0.65, and 0.99, and the implied coefficients are simply these weights multiplied by 0.57. As discussed in the next section, these weights are supported by the data. The main conclusions here are thus that (1) the economy has an effect on the on-term House vote share, (2) the effect is smaller than it is on the presidential vote share, and (3) the weights for the three economic variables are the same as they are for the presidential vote share.

The president running variable has a coefficient of 2.5 with a t-statistic of 2.79, and so it is significant. The incumbent party in the White House has a head start regarding the on-term House vote share of 2.5 percentage points if the president is running for reelection. For the presidential vote share, the head start was 2.9 percentage points.

The coefficient for the party variable is –3.9 with a t-statistic of –4.56. This variable is 1 if the Democratic Party is the incumbent party in the White House and –1 if the Republican Party is the incumbent party in the White House. The coefficient of –3.9 says the following. If the incumbent party is Democratic and if all the other variables are zero, the predicted Democratic vote share is the intercept, 49.6, minus 3.9, or 45.7 percent. If the incumbent party is Republican and if all the other variables are zero, the predicted Democratic vote share is 49.6 plus 3.9, or 53.5 percent. The Republican vote share in this case is 100 minus the predicted Democratic vote share, or 46.5 percent. Therefore, other things being equal, the Republican Party starts off when it is the incumbent party in the White House with a predicted on-term House vote share that is larger than the predicted on-term House vote share for the Democratic Party when it is the incumbent party (46.5 versus 45.7). There is thus a slight bias in favor of the Republican Party, other things being equal.

The coefficient for the war variable is 3.2 with a t-statistic of 1.93. This variable is relevant for only three elections, and it is not very important.

The House vote share lagged has a coefficient of 0.62 with a t-statistic of 5.54. There is thus evidence that the House vote share in the previous midterm election has a positive effect on the on-term House vote share. This is probably the personal incumbency effect at work.

The standard error is 2.1, which is fairly small. From Chapter 2, this means that 68.2 percent of the time the error in predicting the vote share will be between –2.1 and 2.1. The errors in predicting the 24 elections are presented in Table 4-2 along with the actual and predicted

TABLE **4-2** Predicted on-term and midterm House vote shares

	ON-TERM			MIDTERM			
On-Term Year	Actual Vote Share	Predicted Vote Share	Predicted Minus Actual	Actual Vote Share	Predicted Vote Share	Predicted Minus Actual	Midterm Year
1916	48.9	49.4	0.5	45.1	45.1	0.0	1918
1920	38.0	41.5	3.5	46.4	44.8	−1.6	1922
1924	42.1	46.4	4.4	41.6	41.8	0.2	1926
1928	42.8	42.5	−0.3	45.7	48.1	2.4	1930
1932	56.9	54.3	−2.6	56.5	51.0	−5.5	1934
1936	58.5	61.0	2.5	50.8	51.4	0.5	1938
1940	53.0	54.7	1.7	47.7	46.6	−1.0	1942
1944	51.7	51.6	−0.2	45.3	46.3	1.0	1946
1948	53.2	49.8	−3.3	50.0	51.2	1.2	1950
1952	49.9	49.1	−0.9	52.5	52.2	−0.4	1954
1956	51.0	51.0	0.0	56.0	54.3	−1.7	1958
1960	54.8	54.9	0.1	52.5	54.0	1.5	1962
1964	57.3	56.9	−0.5	51.2	52.8	1.5	1966
1968	50.9	51.2	0.3	54.4	53.2	−1.2	1970
1972	52.7	50.9	−1.7	58.5	58.0	−0.5	1974
1976	56.9	57.3	0.5	54.4	52.4	−2.0	1978
1980	51.4	49.4	−1.9	56.0	54.5	−1.5	1982
1984	52.8	50.0	−2.7	55.1	56.0	1.0	1986
1988	54.0	54.6	0.6	54.2	55.7	1.6	1990
1992	52.7	52.5	−0.2	46.5	48.0	1.5	1994
1996	50.2	48.7	−1.4	49.5	47.9	−1.6	1998
2000	49.8	49.5	−0.3	47.6	52.3	4.7	2002
2004	48.6	48.9	0.3	54.1	51.2	−2.9	2006
2008	55.5	57.4	1.9	45.9	48.8	2.9	2010

values. The two largest errors are for 1920, when the Democrats got 38.0 percent and were predicted to get 41.5 percent (error of 3.5), and for 1924, when the Democrats got 42.1 percent and were predicted to get 46.4 percent (error of 4.4). The third largest error is for 1948, when the Democrats got 53.2 percent and were predicted to get 49.8 percent (error of −3.3). All the other errors are less than 3.0 in absolute value.

The overall results thus seem good. There are no very large errors, and the coefficients are significant. In particular, the economy has a significant effect on the vote share.

One other result worth mentioning concerns a possible presidential coattail effect on the on-term House vote share, which was discussed earlier in the chapter. We have seen that the same economic variables affect both the presidential vote share and the on-term House vote share, and so it is obvious why these two vote shares are positively correlated. The question about a presidential coattail effect is whether the presidential vote share independently affects the on-term House vote share. We can test this by simply adding the presidential vote share as an explanatory variable in explaining the on-term House vote share. We did this, and the presidential vote share is not significant. Its coefficient is 0.14 with a t-statistic of 0.77. There is thus no evidence of a presidential coattail effect on the on-term House vote. The presidential vote share does not directly affect the on-term House vote share. The two are positively correlated because they are affected by common explanatory variables.

We now turn to the midterm House vote. The explanatory variables are listed in Box 4-2. The data used are from Table 4-1. The two economic variables, inflation and good news quarters, pertain to the seven quarters before the election. Again, when the incumbent party is Republican, negative values are used for the two economic variables (and thus for index2). The results are shown in Box 4-4.

The coefficient for index2 is 0.72 with a t-statistic of 2.90. The economic variables are thus significant. The coefficient is less than 1.0, which means that the economic variables have a smaller effect on the midterm House vote share than they do on the presidential vote share. The effect is 72 percent of the size of the effect for the presidential vote share. The implied coefficients for inflation and good news quarters are presented at the bottom of Box 4-4. The weights are −0.65 and 0.99, and the implied coefficients are simply these weights multiplied by 0.72.

BOX **4-4**

House midterm vote share depends on:		t-statistic
0.72	index2	2.90
−3.1	party variable	−3.17
1.0	war variable	0.50
0.64	House vote share lagged − 50.0	3.52
−0.33	presidential vote share lagged − 50.0	−2.30
48.5	intercept	69.38
standard error: 2.4		
number of observations: 24		
−0.48	inflation	
0.71	good news quarters	

Again, as discussed in the next section, these weights are supported by the data. The main conclusions for the midterm House vote share are thus the same as they were for the on-term House vote share: (1) the economy has an effect on the midterm House vote share, (2) the effect is smaller than it is on the presidential vote share, and (3) the weights for the two economic variables are the same as they are for the presidential vote share.

The coefficient for the party variable is −3.1 with a t-statistic of −3.17. The coefficient of −3.1 says the following. If the incumbent party in the White House is Democratic and if all the other variables are zero, the predicted Democratic vote share is the intercept, 48.5, minus 3.1, or 45.4 percent. If the incumbent party in the White House is Republican and if all the other variables are zero, the predicted Democratic vote share is 48.5 plus 3.1, or 51.6 percent. The Republican vote share in this case is 100 minus the predicted Democratic vote share, or 48.4 percent. So again, there is a bias of favor of the Republican Party. Other things being equal, it starts off when it is the incumbent party with a predicted midterm House vote share that is larger than the predicted midterm House vote share for the Democratic Party when it is the incumbent party (48.4 versus 45.4).

The coefficient for the party variable is −3.1 with a t-statistic of −3.17. Given this coefficient and given the intercept of 48.5, if all of the other coefficients are zero, the Democratic Party is predicted to receive 48.5 minus 3.1, or 45.4 percent when it is the incumbent party. The Republican Party is predicted to receive 100 minus 48.5 plus 3.1, or 48.4 percent when it is the incumbent party. So again, there is a bias in favor of the Republican Party, other things being equal.

The coefficient for the war variable is 1.0 with a t-statistic of 0.50. It is thus not significant, and it is not very important anyway.

The House vote share lagged has a coefficient of 0.64 with a t-statistic of 3.52. There is thus evidence that the House vote share in the previous on-term election has a positive effect on the midterm House vote share. Again, this is probably the personal incumbency effect at work. It is interesting that the coefficient of 0.64 is essentially the same as the coefficient of 0.62 for the lagged vote share in explaining the on-term House vote share in Box 4-3.

The coefficient for the lagged presidential vote share is −0.33 with a t-statistic of −2.30. As discussed earlier, this is probably picking up a balance effect. It is not an undoing of a positive presidential coattail effect in the previous on-term election because there is no evidence of such an effect.

The standard error is 2.4, which again is fairly small. The errors in predicting the 24 elections are presented in Table 4-2 along with the actual and predicted values. The two largest errors are for 1934, when the Democrats got 56.5 percent and were predicted to get 51.0 percent (error of −5.5), and for 2000, when the Democrats got 47.6 percent and were predicted to get 52.3 percent (error of 4.7). All the other errors are less than 3.0 in absolute value.

The overall results also seem good for the midterm House vote share. There are no very large errors, and the coefficients are significant. In particular, the economy has a significant effect on the vote share.

Possible Pitfalls

Possible pitfalls similar to those for the presidential vote share exist for the House vote shares. Possible data mining, however, may not be quite as serious an issue. The House vote-share analysis was done in 2007, and the only economic variables tried were those that explain the presidential vote share. In fact, as has been discussed, the weights on the economic variables are those that pertain to the presidential vote-share estimates. The only new variables added are the lagged vote shares. On the other hand, the growth rate was not used in the explanation of the midterm House vote because it was not significant. In general, less confidence should probably be placed on the midterm House results than on the on-term House results because there are only seven quarters between the new presidential administration and the midterm House vote.

Although the weights we are using for index1 and index2 might be wrong, we can in fact test whether this is the case or not. The following discussion is more difficult than average, and you may want to skip to the next section. The bottom line is that the data support the use of the weights.

Consider the on-term results in Box 4-3. The main idea of the test is to compare two measures of fit. The first measure is the sum of squared errors that is obtained when index1 is used. Call this *measure A*. The second measure is the sum of squared errors that is obtained when all three economic variables are used separately (in place of index1). Call this *measure B*.

The key point is that measure B is always smaller than measure A. We are allowed more flexibility in fitting the data for measure B because no weighting scheme is forced on the three economic variables. The coefficients of the three variables are those that lead to the smallest sum of squared errors. Now, if the weights are valid, measure B should be only slightly smaller than measure A. On the other hand, if the weights are wrong, measure B is likely to be much smaller than measure A. In this case, measure A is forced to use incorrect weights, and the fit should not be very good. Therefore, if measure A is much larger than measure B, it suggests that the weights are not valid.

The next step is that we need some way to decide when the difference between measures A and B is large and when it is not. Here we need to go back to thinking about different universes, as we did in Chapter 2. Assume that the weights are correct. We know that the size of a typical error is the standard error, which in Box 4-3 is 2.1. If we assume that the errors come from a bell-shaped curve with a standard error of 2.1, we can draw different errors for our second universe. Given these errors, we use the coefficients in Box 4-3 to compute new vote-share values. This drawing is similar to the drawing we discussed in Lesson 4 in Chapter 2 in the sense that we are getting a second universe with different errors and then computing different values of the vote share. Once we have the different vote-share values, we can compute measure A and measure B and then the difference between the two. These values are different from those obtained using the actual universe because we are using different values of the vote share. Remember that we are assuming the weights are valid because we are using the coefficients in Box 4-3, which use the weights, to calculate the vote-share values once the errors have been drawn.

Imagine doing this 1,000 times for 1,000 universes. In the end, we have computed 1,000 differences between measures A and B. The next step is to put these differences in order of their size starting from the largest. We are now almost finished. We take the difference between the two measures that we have computed using the actual data and compare it to the 1,000 differences. Say that this difference is between differences 150 and 151. This says that if the truth is that the weights are valid, we could expect to get a difference as large as ours about 15 percent of the time (150 out of 1,000). This percentage is greater than the usual cutoff of 5 percent, so we would accept the view that the weights are the same. If, on the other hand, the difference in the actual data were between differences 10 and 11, we would reject the view that the weights are valid. In this case, we would expect to get a difference that large only about 1 percent of the time, which is smaller than the 5 percent cutoff.

In practice, tests are a little more complicated than this, and the computations can be done without having to draw errors for other universes. The intuition is, however, the same. The view that the weights are valid is rejected if the difference in fit (that is, the difference between measures like A and B) is large compared to what one would expect to get if the truth were valid weights.

I tested whether the weights are valid, and the case of valid weights was not rejected. This was true both for index1 for the on-term House election and for index2 for the midterm House election. The computed difference between the two measures (measures like A and B) was such that we could expect to get a value as large 91 percent of the time for index1 and 85 percent of the time for index2. These two percentages are much larger than the cutoff of 5 percent.

Real-Time Predictions of the Elections of 2008 and 2010

I have made only two real-time predictions of the House vote shares: the on-term House vote share for 2008 and the midterm House vote share for 2010. These predictions use the coefficients that were available before the election, and they are based on the values of the economic variables that were available right before the election. This is the same procedure that was used for the real-time presidential vote-share predictions in Table 3-3. The real-time predictions are presented in Table 4-3 along with the predictions from Table 4-2.

The actual vote share for 2008 was 55.5 percent, and the real-time prediction was 55.8 percent, for an error of only 0.3 percentage points. The error from Table 4-2 is in fact larger in this case, at 1.9 percentage points. The actual vote share for 2010 was 45.9 percent, and the real-time prediction was 49.2 percent, for an error of 3.3 percentage points. The error from Table 4-2 is 2.9 percentage points. The Democratic share of the House vote fell from 55.5 percent in 2008 to 45.9 percent in 2010, a decline of 9.6 percentage points. This is a large fall. The real-time prediction got about two-thirds of this fall, but not all. Both the errors for 2010 are larger than the standard error of 2.1, but they are not large enough to require a rethinking of the analysis.

Real-Time Predictions for 2012

Table 4-4 presents predictions of the on-term House vote share for 2012 using the three sets of economic values used for the predictions of the presidential vote share in Table 3-4. Under the assumption of a robust

TABLE **4-3**   Real-time and Table 4-2 House vote share predictions: Democratic share of the two-party vote

Year	Actual	REAL-TIME		TABLE 4-2	
		Predicted	Error	Predicted	Error
On-Term House Vote Share					
2008	55.5	55.8	0.3	57.4	1.9
Midterm House Vote Share					
2010	45.9	49.2	3.3	48.8	2.9

TABLE **4-4** Predictions for 2012: Democratic share of two-party on-term House vote

Predicted Share	ECONOMIC VALUES			
	Growth Rate	Inflation	Good News Quarters	
49.9	3.7	1.4	6	Robust economic recovery
46.1	1.0	1.4	1	Modest economic recovery
44.5	−3.0	1.4	1	Double dip recession

recovery in 2011 and 2012, the election is predicted to be essentially a tie—the predicted Democratic share of the two-party House vote is 49.9 percent. For the modest recovery, the Democrats are predicted to get 46.1 percent, and for the double dip recession, they are predicted to get 44.5 percent. Again, alternative predictions can be easily made based on different assumptions about the economic values.

Conclusion

If we consider the overall results of explaining the three vote shares, Boxes 3-2, 4-3, and 4-4, the main conclusions are:

1. There is strong evidence that the economy affects all three vote shares. Not only that, but the relative weights on the economic variables are the same for the presidential and on-term House elections and are the same for two of the three economic variables for the presidential and midterm House elections.
2. There is no evidence of any presidential coattail effects on the on-term House elections. The presidential vote share and the on-term House vote share are highly positively correlated, but this is because they are affected by some of the same variables.
3. The previous midterm House vote share positively affects the on-term House vote share, and the previous on-term House vote share positively affects the midterm House vote share. The coefficients are essentially the same at 0.62 and 0.64.

One explanation for this is a positive incumbency effect for elected representatives.

4. The presidential vote share has a negative effect on the next midterm House vote share. This cannot be due to the reversal of a coattail effect, since there is no evidence of an effect in the first place. Also, it is not simply voting against the party in the White House because the presidential variable is a vote-share variable, not an incumbency variable. The most likely explanation is a balance argument, where voters are reluctant to let one party become too dominant.

You may be tired of politics, so we now turn to sex.

5   Extramarital Affairs

The heavens rejoyce in motion, why should I
Abjure my so much lov'd variety,
And not with many youth and love divide?
Pleasure is none, if not diversifi'd.

    John Donne, Elegie XVII, Variety

We now move from politics to sex, two areas that are sometimes related. Politics and sex are actually related in two ways. One obvious way is that some politicians, including a recent president, engage in extramarital affairs (and sometimes get caught!). The other way is that both how people vote and whether they engage in extramarital affairs are aspects of human behavior that social scientists can attempt to explain. Just as we asked what factors influence how someone votes, we can ask what factors lead someone to have an affair.

Many people engage in extramarital affairs. Most of us probably have at least one friend who we know is having an affair or has had one in the past. A question a social scientist might ask is, what motivates people to have affairs? Just as we examined voting behavior in the last chapter, we can examine affair behavior. In this chapter, we examine the question of what affects a person's behavior regarding the amount of time spent (if any) in an affair.

We begin as usual with a theory—a theory of affair behavior. We next discuss the data that were used to test the theory, and then we test it. Once we have finished with the tests, we can use the results to predict the amount of time (if any) a person with certain characteristics will spend in an affair.

Although this topic may seem unusual for a social scientist to examine, affairs are an important part of many people's lives, and it is of interest to see if any of this behavior can be explained. The topic provides another good example of how the tools in Chapter 2 can be used.

A Theory of Extramarital Affairs

The primary motivation for the theory is the idea that people like variety in their lives. This idea is hardly novel or controversial, and it is easy to find defenses for it. They range from the cliché "variety is the spice of life" to the poem of John Donne at the beginning of this chapter. We will apply this idea to leisure activities, one of which is time spent in an affair.

We begin with the concept of *utility*, which is commonly used in economics to mean satisfaction or happiness. My son gets utility from going to a baseball game. I get utility from running and watching *Antiques Roadshow*. As with satisfaction or happiness, the more utility the better. *Disutility* is negative utility. If we are doing something we don't enjoy, we are said to be getting disutility from it.

The theory begins by considering a married woman, Lynn, and assuming that she can engage in three types of activities: time spent with spouse, time spent with paramour, and time working. (Lynn could be a man: just change *she* to *he* and *her* to *his* in the following discussion.) In the marriage, Lynn gets utility from time spent with her spouse and from the amount of goods consumed with her spouse. In the affair, Lynn gets utility from time spent with her paramour and from the amount of goods consumed with her paramour. Lynn receives two types of income. First, her parents left her a trust fund, and she receives a certain amount of money from it each month, independent of how much she works. This is called her *nonwage income*. Second, she works, and her *wage income* is her wage rate times the number of hours that she works. She uses both of her incomes to buy goods for the marriage and for the affair. The more hours she works, the more income she has to buy goods.

What is Lynn free to decide? There are about 720 hours in a month. She can decide how many of these hours to spend with her spouse, with her paramour, and at work. The total number of hours cannot, of course, exceed the total number of hours in the month. Given the prices of the goods, she also decides how many goods to buy for the marriage and how many for the affair. The total amount that she spends on goods cannot exceed the sum of her nonwage and wage income. (We are assuming no borrowing and no taxes.)

Lynn is assumed to make her decisions so that she receives the largest possible total utility (that is, the utility from the marriage *plus* the utility from the affair). This assumption of utility maximization is common in economics. People are assumed to behave by making themselves as happy or satisfied as possible. (This assumption drives some social scientists nuts—but this is another story.) Lynn is thus assumed to maximize total utility, subject to the constraints that her purchases of goods cannot exceed her nonwage and wage income and that the more she works the less time she has to spend in the marriage and the affair.

We can now consider an important implication from the theory that Lynn behaves by maximizing total utility. What happens if Lynn's aunt dies and leaves her with a second trust, one from which she receives a certain amount of money each month? Her nonwage income rises. Assume that nothing else has changed. Lynn is better off, and when she remaximizes with this higher income, she increases the four things that give her positive utility: time spent with spouse, time spent with paramour, goods consumed in the marriage, and goods consumed in the affair. She works less because she is spending more time in the marriage and the affair. So time spent with paramour will increase when nonwage income increases. We will call this an *income effect*.

What happens if instead Lynn's wage rate increases? You might at first think that the same thing would happen, namely, that she would increase the four things that give her utility, including time spent with paramour. The fact that this may not happen illustrates one of the key insights of economics. This insight concerns the difference between an *income effect* and a *substitution effect*. Say that Lynn's wage rate has doubled from $20 per hour to $40 per hour. Because the reward from working has gone up, Lynn has an incentive to do more of it. Before, when Lynn thought about working an extra hour, she knew she could buy $20 more in goods for the hour worked; now she can buy double this amount. Lynn thus has an incentive to work more because of the extra reward. If she works more, she has less time to spend in the marriage and the affair, so these times will fall. Lynn has "substituted" her time away from the marriage and the affair into work.

There is also, however, something else going on in this case. For any given number of hours worked, Lynn makes more than she did before. Say Lynn worked 160 hours a month before the change, so her wage income was $3,200 a month. If she still worked this amount after her wage rate doubled, her wage income would be $6,400 a month. Her income is thus higher for the same number of hours worked, and we know that, other things being equal, higher income leads her to increase the four things that give her positive utility, including time spent in the marriage and in the affair. If she spends more time with her spouse and with her paramour, she spends less time working. If we focus only on this effect, she will work less than she did before (that is, less than 160 hours a month).

So, what can we say about the effects of an increase in Lynn's wage rate on the amount of time she spends in the affair? We don't know. Lynn is better off because, for a given number of hours worked, she has more income. This alone would lead her to increase all four things. She would buy more goods and spend more time in the marriage and in the affair (and thus also work less). She can both work less and buy more goods because she is making more per hour worked. On the other hand, each hour of work is now more lucrative, and this alone would lead her to work more. If she works more, she spends less time in the marriage and in the affair. The income effect is thus leading her to work less, and the substitution effect is leading her to work more, and the net effect could go either way. If the income effect dominates, she spends less time working and more time in the affair, and if the substitution effect dominates, she spends more time working and less time in the affair.

The key economic insight here is that people may respond differently to an increase in nonwage income than to an increase in the wage rate. A nonwage income increase, such as extra money each month from a trust fund, does not change the amount received for an additional hour worked, and so there is no substitution incentive. There is thus no substitution effect when nonwage income increases, and such an increase has the effect of decreasing the time spent working. People who win big in the lottery usually work less afterward than they otherwise would have. When the wage rate increases, on the other hand, there are both income and substitution effects—the income effect leading to less work and the substitution effect leading to more. The net effect could go either way. People may or may not work less when their wage rate increases.

The income effect and the substitution effect are the two main economic implications of the theory. There are obviously also noneconomic factors at work, and these will be discussed as we present the data.

Anything that has a positive effect on the utility from the marriage leads to less time spent in the affair. Conversely, anything that has a positive effect on the utility from the affair leads to more time spent in the affair.

A person may choose to spend no time in an affair. If Lynn receives no utility (or even negative utility) from an affair under any circumstance, she will spend no time in one. In this case, a change in, say, Lynn's non-wage income will not affect her time spent in an affair, since affair activity never gives her positive utility. The theory does not require that a person spend time in an affair. If a person is having an affair, the theory is concerned with variables that affect the amount of time spent in the affair, but none of these variables matter if a person never receives positive utility from an affair.

The Data

As you might gather, it is not easy to find data to test the theory. The government, for example, does not collect data on extramarital affair activity. The data that were found are from two magazine surveys. The first survey was conducted in 1969 by *Psychology Today (PT)*. A questionnaire on sexual activity was published in the July 1969 issue of *PT*, and readers were asked to mail in their answers. About 20,000 replies were received, of which about 2,000 were coded onto tape. (For young readers: data used to be stored on magnetic tapes for distribution.) The second survey, for women only, was conducted in 1974 by *Redbook (RB)*. A questionnaire on sexual activity was published in the October 1974 issue of *RB*, and readers were asked to mail in their answers. About 100,000 replies were received, of which about 18,000 were coded onto tape. The questionnaires included questions about extramarital affairs as well as about many other aspects of sexual behavior and about various demographic and economic characteristics of the individual.

Table 5-1 lists the variables that were constructed from the data on the two tapes. Only people who were currently married and who had been married only once were included from each tape. People who had been married more than once were excluded because of lack of information on some of the variables for these people. In particular, the question regarding the number of years the person had been married pertains to all marriages; if a person has been married more than once, the length of the

TABLE **5-1** Data for testing the theory of extramarital affairs

Variable	Description	Values	Mean
Psychology Today data (601 observations, 150 where affair is not zero)			
Affair	How often engaged in extramarital sexual intercourse during the past year	0 = none, 1 = once, 2 = twice, 3 = 3 times, 7 = 4−10 times, 12 = monthly, 12 = weekly, 12 = daily	1.46
Years married	No. of years married	.125 = 3 months or less, .417 = 4−6 months, .75 = 6 months−1 year, 1.5 = 1−2 years, 4.0 = 3−5 years, 7.0 = 6−8 years, 10.0 = 9−11 years, 15.0 = 12 or more years	8.18
Age	Age	17.5 = under 20, 22.0 = 20−24, 27.0 = 25−29, 32.0 = 30−34, 37.0 = 35−39, 42.0 = 40−44, 47.0 = 45−49, 52.0 = 50−54, 57.0 = 55 or over	32.5
Marital happiness	How rate marriage	5 = very happy, 4 = happier than average, 3 = average, 2 = somewhat unhappy, 1 = very unhappy	3.93
Religiosity	How religious	5 = very, 4 = somewhat, 3 = slightly, 2 = not at all, 1 = anti	3.12
Occupation	Occupation	Values between 1 and 7, ranked by social position of occupation	4.19
Redbook data (6,355 observations, 2,053 where affair is not zero)			
Affair	Measure of time spent in extramarital affairs	Equal to 0 if no sexual relations with man other than husband; otherwise equal to (no. men × frequency)/years married. (Values range from 0 to 57.6)	0.705
No. men	If since marriage have had sexual relations with man other than husband, with how many different men	1.0 = 1, 3.5 = 2−5, 8.0 = 6−10, 12.0 = more than 10	N/A

TABLE **5-1** Data for testing the theory of extramarital affairs (*continued*)

Variable	Description	Values	Mean
Redbook data (6,355 observations, 2,053 where affair is not zero)			
Frequency	Continuing from previous question, approximate number of times had sexual relations with each man	1.0 = once, 3.5 = 2−5, 8.0 = 6−10, 12.0 = more than 10, 5.6 = it varied greatly from partner to partner	N/A
Years married	No. years married	.5 = less than 1 year, 2.5 = 1−4 years, 6.0 = 5−7 years, 9.0 = 8−10 years, 13.0 if more than 10 years and oldest child is under 12 years of age, 16.5 if more than 10 years and oldest child is between 12 and 17 years of age, 23.0 if more than 10 years and oldest child is 18 years of age or over	9.01
Age	Age	17.5 = under 20, 22.0 = 20−24, 27.0 = 25−29, 32.0 = 30−34, 37.0 = 35−39, 42.0 = 40 or over	29.1
Marital happiness	How rate marriage	5 = very good, 4 = good, 3 = fair, 2 = poor, 1 = very poor	4.11
Religiosity	How religious	4 = strongly, 3 = fairly, 2 = mildly, 1 = not	2.43
Occupation	Occupation	6 = professional with advanced degree, 5 = managerial, administrative, business, 4 = teacher, counselor, social worker, nurse; artist, writer; technician, skilled worker, 3 = white-collar (sales, clerical, secretarial), 2 = farming, agriculture; semi-skilled or unskilled worker; other, 1 = student	3.42

current marriage cannot be determined. Also, only people who were employed were included from each tape. Unemployed people were excluded because the theory does not necessarily pertain to them. The theory pertains to people deciding how much time to work versus how much time to spend doing other things, and people who are not working at all are a special case and are to some extent outside the theory. Also excluded from the tapes were people who failed to answer all the relevant questions.

After these exclusions, there were 601 observations left from the *PT* tape. Of these, 150 (25.0 percent) had at least one affair during the past year. There were 6,366 observations left from the *RB* tape. Of these, 2,053 (32.2 percent) had at least one affair since the person's marriage.

Table 5-1 lists each variable and how it was constructed. In the Values column, the items to the right of the equal sign are the answers that were allowed on the questionnaires. The numbers to the left of the equal sign are the values that I chose to represent the answer. A number of questions were open-ended in the upper range, and in each of these cases, I had to make a fairly arbitrary choice for the largest value of the variable.

The *RB* questionnaire did not ask if the person was currently having an affair. The affair variable that was used in this case was taken to be the number of different men with whom the woman had sexual relations since the marriage times the frequency with each man, and then this was divided by the number of years married. This affair variable is at least a rough measure of the time spent in extramarital affairs.

The one economic variable from each tape is occupation. Each occupation is assigned a number based primarily on social position—the larger the number, the higher the social position. We will use this variable as a proxy for the person's wage rate, but it is at best a rough approximation. The ranking of jobs by social position is not exactly the same as the ranking of jobs by the size of the wage rate, so the occupation variable is not a perfect measure of the person's wage rate. It is, unfortunately, all we have.

We will test the theory by estimating coefficients for the variables shown in Box 5-1. What does the theory say about these variables? If we assume that occupation is a proxy for the person's wage rate, then the theory says that occupation is likely to have an effect on the affair variable, but whether the effect is positive or negative is ambiguous. If the income effect dominates, the effect is positive, and if the substitution effect dominates, the effect is negative.

BOX **5-1**

affair depends on:	
	occupation
	years married
	age
	marital happiness
	religiosity

If the number of years married has a negative effect on the utility from the marriage because of boredom, then the years married variable should have a positive effect on the affair. Remember that the individual (Lynn) is maximizing total utility—the utility from the marriage plus the utility from the affair—and if utility from the marriage is low because of boredom, total utility will be maximized by spending more time in the affair than otherwise.

If age has a negative effect on the enjoyment of sexual activity, something that may or may not be true (see Chapter 8 for estimates of how fast people slow down), and if affairs are primarily sexual, then age will have a negative effect on the utility from the affair. If the utility from the affair is low because of small sexual pleasure, total utility will be maximized by spending less time in the affair than otherwise.

If marital happiness has a positive effect on the utility from the marriage (which seems obvious), then it should have a negative effect on the affair. For a happily married person, total utility will be maximized by spending more time in the marriage than otherwise.

If a person's religious intensity has a negative effect on the utility from the affair, then the religiosity variable should have a negative effect on the affair. A religious person may be concerned about possible divine disapprobation from engaging in an affair, and he or she may not feel good about having one, or at least about spending much time in one.

Fit and Test

We are now ready to estimate the coefficients and their t-statistics. Once again, we use a computer to find the set of coefficients that gives the best fit—the smallest sum of squared errors. The one new wrinkle concerns the large number of zero values for the affair variable. If someone is not having an affair, he or she may not be close to starting one. (As has been discussed, the person may receive no utility from an affair under any circumstances.) For this person, a decrease in, say, religious intensity is unlikely to lead the person to begin an affair. This is in contrast to someone who is already having an affair, where a decrease in religious intensity may lead the person to spend at least a little more time in the affair.

There are thus, to some extent, two types of people: those who are unlikely to be moved from zero by at least modest changes in the explanatory variables and those who are not at zero and may change the amount of time in the affair as the explanatory variables change. We thus need to account for the fact that things are different when the value of the dependent variable is zero from when it is above zero. There are methods that take into account this difference, and I have used one of these methods here. It is still the case that a type of best fit is obtained. It is just that the measure of how well a set of coefficients fits the data is not exactly the sum of the squared errors. The insights from Chapter 2, however, are still relevant. (It is beyond the scope of this book to discuss this method.)

The results for the two surveys are shown in Boxes 5-2 and 5-3. Let's look at the occupation variable first. It has a positive coefficient in both cases. It is significant for the *Redbook* data, but it only has a *t*-statistic of 1.29 for the *Psychology Today* data. The results are thus mixed, but there is at least some evidence that occupation has a positive

BOX **5-2**

Psychology Today data		*t*-statistic
affair depends on:		
0.326	occupation	1.29
0.554	years married	4.13
−0.179	age	−2.26
−2.28	marital happiness	−5.61
−1.69	religiosity	−4.14
8.17	intercept	2.96
standard error: 2.87		
number of observations: 601		

BOX **5-3**

Redbook data		
affair depends on:		t-statistic
0.255	occupation	3.30
0.140	years married	6.11
−0.120	age	−4.91
−1.53	marital happiness	−20.82
−0.950	religiosity	−11.14
7.18	intercept	11.39
standard error: 2.12		
number of observations: 6,366		

effect on an affair. To the extent that the occupation variable is a proxy for the wage rate, the positive effect means that the income effect dominates the substitution effect. A high wage person relative to a low wage person, other things equal, works less and spends more time in an affair.

The other coefficients have the expected sign and are significant. The number of years married has a positive effect on an affair (the boredom effect), and age has a negative effect (the physical slowing down effect). Marital happiness has a negative effect, as expected, and the religiosity variable has a negative effect, again as expected if there is a fear of divine disapprobation by religious people.

As with many studies in social science, the testing of the present theory is limited by the quality of the data. An important test of the theory would be to have a measure of nonwage income. The theory says that nonwage income should have an unambiguously positive effect on time spent in the affair. Unfortunately, we have no such variable to include, and this aspect of the theory cannot be tested.

Data existed on the level of education of the person and the number of children in the marriage. These two variables were added, and neither was significant for either data set. The lack of significance of the education variable is perhaps not surprising, since there is no particular reason to expect that the level of education of a person affects the utility from the marriage and the utility from the affair differently. On the other hand, one might expect the number of children to increase the utility from the marriage and thus for the number of children to have a negative effect on time spent in the affair. Since the number of children was not significant in either data set, there is no evidence that this is true. Children seem to be a wash, at least in these two data sets.

Possible Pitfalls

As discussed in the previous section, the lack of data on nonwage income limits the testing of the economic implications of the theory. Also, the occupation variable is at best only a crude measure of a person's wage rate. Better tests could be made with better data. The quality of the data is something that you should keep in mind in deciding how much to trust the current results.

The rest of this section is hard, and it can be skipped if desired. It concerns an important and difficult problem that arises in social science research: selection bias. It will take some time to explain what this means. We will take a simple example to illustrate the point. We will assume that the time spent in an affair depends only on marital happiness. Figure 5-1 is a graph of hypothetical data, with time spend in an affair on the vertical axis and marital happiness on the horizontal axis. Let's also forget the zero problem and assume that everyone is spending at least a little time in an affair. (Selection bias can exist with or without any zeros.)

Figure 5-1 shows the best fitting line using all the points in the figure. There are a number of points for people with a marital happiness value of 5, a number for those with a value of 4, and similarly for values of 3, 2, and 1. The line is downward sloping: the happier one is in the marriage, the smaller the amount of time spent in the affair.

Let's first consider what is *not* a problem. It is all right if we do not have a random sample of the population regarding the degree of marital happiness. Say that our sample contains a much larger fraction of unhappily married people than is true in the total population. (Perhaps *Psychology Today* and *Redbook* readers are on average less happily married than is the total population.) All this means regarding Figure 5-1 is that we have an unrepresentatively large number of points for marital happiness of 1 and 2 and an unrepresentatively small number of points for marital happiness of 4 and 5. There is, however, no bias when we find the best

Affair

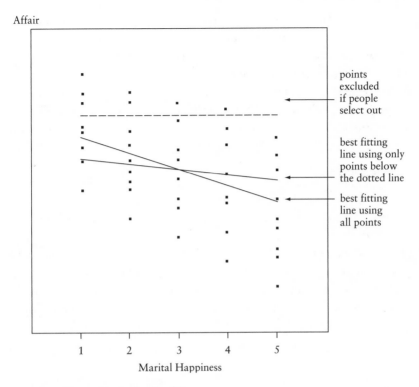

points
excluded
if people
select out

best fitting
line using only
points below
the dotted line

best fitting
line using
all points

1   2   3   4   5

Marital Happiness

FIGURE **5-1**   Example of selection bias

fitting line using our data. Just because we have a relatively large number of observations for a particular happiness level does not mean that the points we have are on average too high or too low. Remember that the distance from a point to the line is an *error*. In the present context, an error reflects all the things that affect time spent in an affair aside from marital happiness. For any sample of people of, say, happiness level 4, some are above the line and some are below the line, but there is no reason to think that more are above than below. You can think about the errors for these people as being drawn randomly from a bell-shaped curve like that in Figure 2-2. Nothing that was said in Chapter 2 requires that we have a representative sample. It thus does not matter that the *Psychology Today* and *Redbook* readers are unlikely to be a representative sample of the total population regarding variables like marital happiness (that is, the explanatory variables).

So, what is the selection bias problem? This problem occurs if people choose to answer the questionnaire based on how much time they are spending in an affair. It may be, for example, that people who spend little time in an affair don't find the questionnaire as interesting and are thus less inclined to fill it out than those who are quite active in an affair. Or perhaps people who are quite active in an affair are less inclined to fill out the questionnaire for fear of arousing suspicion from a possibly already suspicious spouse. In either case, our estimate of the slope will be wrong (biased).

To take a specific example, consider all the points above the dotted line in Figure 5-1. These are people who spend considerable time in an affair. You can see that more of the points occur for people who have a low marital happiness rating (1 or 2) than those who have a high rating (4 or 5). This, of course, is as expected. We are much less likely to find a happily married person spending a large amount of time in an affair than we are to find an unhappily married person spending a large amount of time in one. Another way of looking at this is that the error for a happily married person spending a large amount of time in an affair is large, and large errors are less likely to be drawn from a bell-shaped curve than are small ones.

Now let's say that no one above the dotted line fills out the questionnaire for fear of getting caught. When we collect the data, we thus see only those points below the dotted line. What happens when we find the best fitting line using only the points below the dotted line? It should not be surprising that the slope of the line changes. In this case, the slope would get flatter, as shown in Figure 5-1. We have excluded more high points around happiness levels 1 and 2 than around 4 and 5, and this distorts the best fitting line. The slope is wrong, or biased. This in a nutshell is the selection bias problem.

To summarize, the selection bias problem arises when the choice of whether a person participates in a study depends on the size of the dependent variable.

Is selection bias likely to be a problem in the *PT* and *RB* data? As previously discussed, one can tell plausible sounding stories in both directions—people who are very active selecting out and people who are very inactive selecting out. This is to some extent good, since there is no strong argument for one side only. There is no real way of knowing, however, and so selection bias is another possible pitfall that you must keep in the back of your mind when judging the results.

There is one last point on the sample. Earlier, we discussed why it is not a problem if the *Psychology Today* and *Redbook* readers are not a representative sample of the total population as long as there is no selection bias. When we say this, however, we are assuming that the coefficients are the same for everyone in the population. People can differ in the values of the explanatory variables but not in the coefficients that are attached to these variables. If the coefficients differ among individuals, we are in a different ball game. If coefficients differ across groups of individuals, such as *Psychology Today* and *Redbook* readers versus *Field and Stream* readers, we must treat each group separately in the sense of finding the best fitting set of coefficients group by group. We cannot combine the groups and find the best fitting set of coefficients because no such set exists.

Examine the Results and Predict

To the extent we can trust the results, how can we use them? The results say that the amount of time spent in an affair depends positively on the person's occupation (wage rate) and number of years married. It depends negatively on the person's age, marital happiness, and religious intensity. We can thus say that if we know someone who (1) has a high wage rate, (2) has been married a long time, (3) is fairly young given the length of time he or she has been married, (4) is unhappily married, and (5) is not religious, then this person is a likely candidate for spending considerable time in an affair. We can thus get from the results a sense of who is and who is not likely to have an active affair life.

We can also make quantitative statements using the size of the coefficients. The following numbers are approximately correct for people who are already spending time in an affair and are not close to the margin of ending the affair (see the Notes to this chapter for more details). The numbers are not accurate for people who are not currently in an affair or are in an affair but are close to the margin of ending it.

Consider the *PT* results first. If the number of years married increases by 10 years, the affairs variable increases by 5.54 (the coefficient of 0.554 times 10). An extra 10 years of marriage thus increases the number of affair encounters a year by between 5 and 6. On the other hand, an increase in a person's age by 10 years decreases the number of encounters by 1.79, or about 2 a year. If marital happiness decreases from happier than average (rating 4) to somewhat unhappy (rating 2), the number of encounters increases by 4.56, or between 4 and 5 a year. If the religiosity variable decreases from somewhat (rating 4) to not at all (rating 2), the number of encounters increases by 3.38, or about 3 a year.

We can do the same thing for the *RB* results. An extra 10 years of marriage leads to an increase of 1.4 encounters a year. An extra 10 years of age leads to a decrease of 1.2 encounters a year. A 2-point drop in marital happiness leads to an increase of 3.06 encounters a year. A 2-point drop in religiosity leads to an increase of 1.9 encounters a year.

These kinds of statements are, of course, of limited interest because there is no specific person we are talking about. They do, however, give you a sense of magnitudes.

Conclusion

How many chapters on sex have you read where you learned about income and substitution effects as well as selection bias, not to mention the use of interesting statistical tools? But enough of sex and lemans; we are now on to wine.

6   Wine Quality

A cup of wine that's brisk and fine,
And drink unto the leman mine;
And a merry heart lives long-a
    William Shakespeare, from King Henry IV—Part II

This chapter will make some wine connoisseurs angry. We will show that the tools in Chapter 2 can be used to explain and predict wine quality. Some people feel that wine quality is too subtle to be quantified. How can a social scientist, who may not know a Bordeaux from a Burgundy, explain and predict wine quality better than wine experts? This chapter shows how. It is based on a fascinating (to me at least) article by Orley Ashenfelter, David Ashmore, and Robert Lalonde, "Bordeaux Wine Vintage Quality and the Weather," *Chance* (1995): 7–14. (I am indebted to the authors for supplying me with their data.)

In what follows, *vintage* means the year in which the wine was bottled and *wine quality* means the quality the wine ultimately attains after it has properly aged. Keep in mind that the quality a wine ultimately attains is not known with certainty at the time it is bottled. Generally, young wines don't taste very good, and it takes years to know for sure how good the wine is.

We will deal in this chapter with red Bordeaux wines from the top châteaux (vineyards). There is nothing in the following analysis, however, that prevents the procedure from being used for other types of wines.

Theory and Data

The theory is very simple. It is that wine quality depends on the weather in the harvest year. The best conditions are when (1) the growing season (April–September) is warm, (2) August and September are dry, and (3) the previous winter (October–March) has been wet. This is a theory that most people, including wine experts, accept. Casual observation reveals that the great Bordeaux vintages have corresponded to warm growing seasons, dry Augusts and Septembers, and previous wet winters.

You should now have had enough experience from the previous chapters to see where we might go with this. If we can get a measure of wine quality and if we can get measures of the weather in the Bordeaux region of France, we can use the weather variables to help explain the wine quality variable.

The first step is to get a measure of wine quality. In 1855, the châteaux in the Médoc region of Bordeaux were ranked by quality and put into five classes, with the top châteaux receiving a *premiers crus* rating. This ranking was based on the price of the wine. Châteaux with the highest prices for their wines were given the premiers crus rating, châteaux with slightly lower prices were given the next ranking (*seconds crus*), and so on. Using prices to measure quality seems perfectly sensible. The better a wine, the higher we would expect its price to be.

We will deal with six châteaux. The ranking of these six using today's prices is Latour, Lafite, Cheval Blanc, Pichon-Lalande, Cos d'Estournel, and Montrose. The 1855 classification of these wines has held up fairly well over time. The ranking in 1855 was Lafite, Latour, Pichon-Lalande, Cos d'Estournel, and Montrose. (Cheval Blanc was not ranked in 1855.) Latour and Lafite were ranked premiers crus in 1855, and Pichon-Lalande, Cos d'Estournel, and Montrose were ranked seconds crus.

The reason wine quality varies across châteaux has to do with the geography of the vineyard. The best wines are produced on a slope with a southern exposure to the sun and in soil with good drainage. Although it is interesting to compare wines of the same vintage across châteaux, such as comparing a 1966 Latour to a 1966 Montrose, this is not the subject matter of this chapter. (As just noted, differences across châteaux primarily reflect differences in the geography of the vineyards.) We are instead interested in the prices of different vintages from the same chateau. How does, say, a 1961 Lafite compare to a 1963 Lafite? The theory says that this difference should depend on the weather in 1961 versus 1963.

Wines trade in secondary (auction) markets, with one of the main markets located in London, so it is possible to get data on prices of wines by chateau and vintage from these markets. We can, for example, get the price of a 1961 Lafite, a 1962 Lafite, a 1961 Latour, a 1962 Latour, and so on. Since we are interested in different years, one possibility for a price variable would simply be to take a particular chateau, say, Latour, and use the prices of the Latour vintages. The price variable actually used, however, is a weighted average of the prices of the six châteaux listed earlier. For example, the price used for the 1966 vintage is a weighted average of the six châteaux prices for the 1966 vintage. By not relying solely on one chateau, this procedure probably gives slightly better estimates of the price differences across vintage years. The six châteaux were chosen because they are large producers and their wines appear frequently in the auction markets. The prices were the ones recorded in London in 1990–1991.

Regarding the weather variables, data on Bordeaux's weather are readily available from historical records. Three measures of weather have been used: (1) the average temperature in April–September, (2) the amount of rain in August and September, and (3) the amount of rain in the preceding October–March period.

The theory is that vintage price depends on the three weather variables. One other variable is also likely to matter, which is the age of the vintage. It costs money to store wines, and so, other things being equal, older wines should sell for more than younger ones to compensate people for the extra holding period. The theory is summarized in Box 6-1.

BOX **6-1**

vintage price depends on:	
	temperature April–Sept.
	rainfall Aug.–Sept.
	rainfall previous Oct.–March
	age of vintage

The data are presented in Table 6-1. The vintage years are from 1952 through 1980, with 1954 and 1956 excluded because of insufficient data. (By 1990, the 1954 and 1956 vintages were no longer traded much;

TABLE **6-1**   Data for explaining wine prices

Vintage	Price (1961 = 1.000)	Temp. Average April–Sept. (°C)	Total Rainfall Aug.–Sept. (mL)	Rainfall Previous Oct.–March (mL)	Age (1983 = 0)
1952	0.368	17.12	160	600	31
1953	0.635	16.73	80	690	30
1955	0.446	17.15	130	502	28
1957	0.221	16.13	110	420	26
1958	0.180	16.42	187	582	25
1959	0.658	17.48	187	485	24
1960	0.139	16.42	290	763	23
1961	1.000	17.33	38	830	22
1962	0.331	16.30	52	697	21
1963	0.168	15.72	155	608	20
1964	0.306	17.27	96	402	19
1965	0.106	15.37	267	602	18
1966	0.473	16.53	86	819	17
1967	0.191	16.23	118	714	16
1968	0.105	16.20	292	610	15
1969	0.117	16.55	244	575	14
1970	0.404	16.67	89	622	13
1971	0.272	16.77	112	551	12
1972	0.101	14.98	158	536	11
1973	0.156	17.07	123	376	10
1974	0.111	16.30	184	574	9
1975	0.301	16.95	171	572	8
1976	0.253	17.65	247	418	7
1977	0.107	15.58	87	821	6
1978	0.270	15.82	51	763	5
1979	0.214	16.17	122	717	4
1980	0.136	16.00	74	578	3

they were not very good.) There are thus 27 observations. The table lists the price variable, the three weather variables, and the vintage age variable. The price variable is the price of the vintage relative to the price of the 1961 vintage. The 1966 price of .473, for example, means that the 1966 vintage sold for 47.3 percent of the 1961 vintage.

The 1961 vintage was truly outstanding—the best of the 27 vintages in the table in terms of price. You can see that the weather was excellent in 1961. The temperature in April–September was very warm (17.33 degrees centigrade); there was almost no rainfall in August–

September (38 milliliters); and there was considerable rainfall in the previous October–March (830 milliliters). It doesn't get much better than this. A real dog was 1968, with a fairly cold growing season (16.20 degrees centigrade), considerable rainfall in August–September (292 milliliters), and modest rainfall in the previous winter (610 milliliters). The price of the 1968 vintage is only 10.5 percent of the 1961 vintage price!

You may examine Table 6-1 for more examples if you wish, but our concern now is to find the set of coefficients that best explains the price. This is done in the next section.

Fit the Data

The dependent variable is the vintage price, and the explanatory variables are the four variables in Box 6-1 plus the intercept. The procedure is the same as in Chapter 2: we find the best fitting set of coefficients and then compute the t-statistics. The vintage price variable that is used for these calculations is in percentage terms. (To be more precise, the price variable used is the logarithm of the price variable in Table 6-1, although it is not really necessary to know this. The main point is that the price variable used in the estimation is in percentage terms.) The results are presented in Box 6-2.

BOX **6-2**

vintage price depends on:		t-statistic
.617	temperature April–Sept.	6.49
−.00387	rainfall Aug.–Sept.	−4.80
.00117	rainfall previous Oct.–March	2.43
.0239	age of vintage	3.34
−12.16	intercept	−7.21
standard error: 0.286		
number of observations: 27		

The three weather variables are significant and have the expected signs, and so this is support for the theory. The temperature in April–September has a positive coefficient and a t-statistic of 6.49. Rainfall in August–September has a negative coefficient and a t-statistic of –4.80.

And rainfall in the previous October–March has a positive coefficient and a *t*-statistic of 2.43. The vintage age variable is also significant. The coefficient of .0239 says that, other things being equal, a vintage price rises 2.39 percent per year.

To see how well the vintage price has been explained, we have listed the predicted and actual values in Table 6-2 for each of the 27 vintage years. The predicted values in Table 6-2 are based on the use of the actual values of the weather variables. Table 6-2 is similar to Table 3-2, which listed the predicted and actual values of the vote share. The vintage price variable that is used in Table 6-2 is the same as the one in Table 6-1.

TABLE **6-2**   Actual versus predicted wine prices by vintage

Vintage	Actual Price (1961 = 1.000)	Predicted Price	Percentage Error
1952	0.368	0.463	0.229
1953	0.635	0.538	−0.166
1955	0.446	0.439	−0.015
1957	0.221	0.219	−0.009
1958	0.180	0.230	0.243
1959	0.658	0.385	−0.536
1960	0.139	0.182	0.268
1961	1.000	0.891	−0.115
1962	0.331	0.374	0.121
1963	0.168	0.154	−0.085
1964	0.306	0.387	0.235
1965	0.106	0.076	−0.328
1966	0.473	0.396	−0.178
1967	0.191	0.251	0.273
1968	0.105	0.109	0.034
1969	0.117	0.152	0.263
1970	0.404	0.308	−0.272
1971	0.272	0.269	−0.011
1972	0.101	0.072	−0.344
1973	0.156	0.241	0.435
1974	0.111	0.146	0.272
1975	0.301	0.223	−0.300
1976	0.253	0.209	−0.192
1977	0.107	0.169	0.457
1978	0.270	0.206	−0.273
1979	0.214	0.179	−0.177
1980	0.136	0.161	0.171

It is the ratio of each vintage price to the 1961 vintage price. Each error in the table is the percentage error. For example, for 1952, the actual price is 0.368, the predicted price is 0.463, and the percentage error is 0.229 (22.9 percent). (To be precise, the percentage error is the logarithm of the predicted price minus the logarithm of the actual price, but it is not necessary to know this.) Note that the standard error from Box 6-2 is 0.286 (28.6 percent), which means that on average we should see an error of roughly that size.

The largest error in the table is for 1959. The actual price is .658, which is quite high, but the predicted price is only .385. The percent error is −0.536—more than a −50 percent error. You can see from Table 6-1 that in 1959 the April–September temperature was quite warm, which is good, but there was a lot of rain in August–September and less rain than average in the previous October–March, both of which are not good. The net effect is that the 1959 vintage is not predicted to be nearly as good as it was.

There are two errors larger than 40 percent in Table 6-2. These are 43.5 percent for 1973 and 45.7 percent for 1977. Each of these vintages is priced low. The percentage errors are graphed in Figure 6-1, where you can easily see these two errors.

Overall, the results seem fairly good. The three weather variables are significant, and their coefficients are of the expected signs. The standard error is 0.286 so that about 68 percent of the time we can expect an error in predicting the price between −28.6 and 28.6 percent.

Possible Pitfalls

Probably, the main possible pitfall is that the weather variables may be too simple to capture adequately the subtle effects of the weather on wine quality. Only three variables are used for the entire year, and possibly, more are needed. The authors of this study did try a fourth weather variable, the average temperature in September of the harvest year, but it was not significant. It still may be, however, that other measures of the weather would improve the fit (that is, lower the standard error).

It is important to note that if variables that help explain wine prices have been omitted, there is unlikely to be omitted variable bias for the three included weather variables. For there to be omitted variable

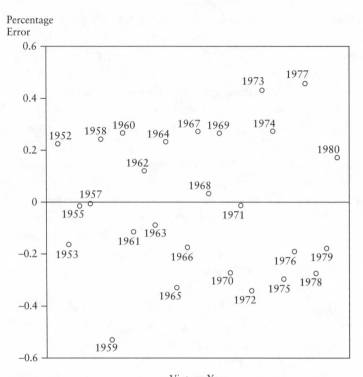

FIGURE **6-1**   Percentage errors predicting wine prices

bias, the included variables must be correlated with the omitted variables. The weather variables are not affected by anything that humans do (well, at least not in the short run) and are not likely to be correlated with anything. Therefore, even if variables have been omitted that should not be, the coefficients of the included weather variables will not be biased.

Returning to possible pitfalls, there is the possibility of data mining. If the authors tried many weather variables and picked the three that gave the best fit, the results may be a fluke. In other words, the three weather variables may fit the data well for the particular 27 vintage years but may not in fact capture well the ways in which weather affects wine quality. We will do a test for this in the next section.

Another potentially serious pitfall is that prices may not accurately reflect quality. If a particular wine becomes "hot" for some faddish reason that has nothing to do with the quality of the wine, its price may rise way above what its true quality would dictate. That is, there could be conspicuous consumption effects on wine prices independent of quality. There is currently, for example, a very influential wine critic, Robert Parker, whose views on wines seem to affect their prices. If Parker is sometimes wrong about a wine's quality (no one is perfect) and if his ratings affect prices, then a wine's price may deviate from its true quality. We will have more to say about this issue in the next section, where an alternative measure of quality is discussed.

I said at the beginning of this chapter that using statistical tools to predict wine quality would make some wine connoisseurs angry. Can three weather variables really do all the work? You know now, of course, that fits are not perfect in the sense that generally there are errors. The weather variables clearly cannot do all the work, and we have seen that the standard error is 28.6 percent. Some people don't understand errors of this sort, and an amusing example concerns a comment that appeared in the magazine *The Wine Spectator* on the attempt of the authors of the journal article to explain wine quality.

> The theory depends for its persuasiveness on the match between vintage quality as predicted by climate data and vintage price on the auction market. But the predictions come out exactly true only 3 times in the 27 vintages since 1961 that he's calculated, even though the formula was specifically designed to fit price data that already existed. The predicted prices are both under and over the actual prices.

(The vintages actually begin in 1952, not 1961.) As my children said when they were younger, duh!

Predict

An interesting test of the theory is to use the coefficients in Box 6-2 to predict vintage prices beyond 1980, the last vintage in the sample. Let's focus on five vintages: 1987, 1988, 1989, 1990, and 1991. Table 6-3 presents data on the three weather variables for each of these vintages. The age variable is also presented in the table. The age variable is taken to be 0 in 1983 (see Table 6-1), so its values for 1987 and beyond are negative. The age variable is a counting variable, and it does not matter

TABLE **6-3**   Data for predicting wine prices, 1987–1991

Vintage	Temp. April–Sept. (°C)	Total Rainfall Aug.–Sept. (mL)	Rainfall Previous Oct.–March (mL)	Age (1983 = 0)
1987	16.98	115	452	−4
1988	17.10	59	808	−5
1989	18.60	82	443	−6
1990	18.70	80	468	−7
1991	17.70	183	570	−8

which year is taken to be 0. All that matters is that the variable changes by 1 each year, which it does.

We can use the values of the weather variables and the coefficients in Box 6-2 to predict the vintage price for each of the five years. These predictions are based on the actual values of the explanatory variables, but they use coefficients that have only been estimated using data up to 1980. If data mining is a serious problem, these predictions should not generally be very good because the 1987–1991 observations have not been used to obtain the coefficients. In fact, the predictions are 8 to 12 years beyond the end of the sample.

The predictions are presented in Table 6-4. You can see that the most expensive vintage is predicted to be 1990, which is predicted to sell at 57.8 percent of the 1961 vintage price. (Remember that we are always dealing with prices relative to the 1961 price.) The next most expensive is 1989 at 53.6 percent and then 1988 at 36.4 percent. The vintages 1987 and 1991 are not predicted to be very good, at 18.4 and 23.1 percent.

It is easy to see from Table 6-3 why the 1989 and 1990 vintages are predicted to be so good. The harvest season was very warm (18.60 and 18.70 degrees centigrade), and there was little rain in August and September (82 and 80 milliliters). On the other hand, the previous October–March periods were not all that wet (443 and 468 milliliters), so the predicted price was high but not close to the 1961 price. You can also see why the 1987 vintage is not predicted to be very good: not a particularly warm harvest season, considerable rain in August and September, and not much rain the previous October–March.

TABLE **6-4**   Predicted wine prices by vintage, 1987–1991

Vintage	Predicted Price (1961 = 1.000)
1987	0.184
1988	0.364
1989	0.536
1990	0.577
1991	0.230

TABLE **6-5**   Wine prices per bottle on August 22, 2001

	1961	1987	1988	1989	1990	1991
[.50ex] Latour	$1,500	$115	$140	$185	$400	$90
Lafite	700	80	165	190	225	75
Cheval Blanc	800	85	145	185	500	75
Pichon-Lalande	275	40	90	140	90	40
Cos d'Estournel	275	35	75	100	125	35
Montrose	225	30	45	95	225	35
Average (all 6)	629.17	64.16	110.00	149.17	260.83	58.33
Average (last 3)	258.33	35.00	70.00	111.67	146.67	36.67

NOTE: Prices obtained from Mt. Carmel Wine & Spirits, Hamden, CT.

To evaluate these predictions, we need to decide what to compare the predictions to. The source of the vintage price data through 1980 was 1990–1991 London auction prices, and 1990–1991 is too soon for the 1987–1991 vintages. (Remember that it takes a number of years before the true quality of a vintage is known.) To get some actual prices, on August 22, 2001, I called a local wine merchant in the New Haven, Connecticut, area and inquired about wine prices for these vintages. These prices are in Table 6-5.

You can see that the prices range from $1,500 per bottle for a 1961 Latour to $30 for a 1987 Montrose. Aside from 1961, the most expensive wine is a 1990 Cheval Blanc at $500. Two averages are presented in Table 6-5. The first is the average across all six châteaux, and the second is the average across the last three. If there is a problem of conspicuous consumption or faddish buying, it seems more likely to show up in the prices for the very top châteaux than for the next group down. (Remember the last three châteaux are all seconds crus. Who can impress one's neighbors with merely a seconds cru?)

Now comes the punch line. We can compare the actual prices in Table 6-5 with the predicted prices in Table 6-4. The comparison is in Table 6-6. Table 6-6 requires a little explanation. The predicted values in Table 6-6 are from Table 6-4, and they are predicted prices relative to the 1961 price. The first column of actual values is based on the average of all six prices in Table 6-5. The 1987 value of .102, for example, is the ratio of 64.16 to 629.17. The 1988 value of .175 is the ratio of 110.00 to 629.17 and so on. The percentage errors using these actual values are presented in the next column. (Again, a percentage error is the logarithm of the predicted price minus the logarithm of the actual price.) The next column of actual values is based on the average of the last three châteaux's prices in Table 6-5. The 1987 value of .135 is the ratio of 35.00 to 258.33, the 1988 value of .271 is the ratio of 70.00 to 258.33, and so on. The percentage errors using these actual values are presented in the last column.

Table 6-6 contains a remarkable result. The average percentage error using the actual prices of the last three châteaux is .265, which is slightly smaller than the standard error of .286. Even though we are about a decade away from the end of the sample period, the predicted values are in line with what we would expect if the theory were accurate. The ranking of the five vintage years is the same for both the predicted and actual values that are based on the last three châteaux: 1990, 1989, 1988, 1991, and 1987. If we stopped here, it would probably be cause for celebration—bring out a 1990 Pichon-Lalande!

TABLE **6-6**   Predicted wine prices by vintage, 1987–1991

Vintage	Predicted Price	Actual Price (all 6)	Percentage Error	Actual Price (last 3)	Percentage Error
1987	.184	.102	.590	.135	.310
1988	.364	.175	.732	.271	.295
1989	.536	.237	.816	.432	.216
1990	.578	.415	.331	.568	.017
1991	.231	.093	.910	.142	.487
Average			.676		.265

NOTE: 1961 = 1.000

Alas, there is a fly in the ointment. If we use all six châteaux's prices, the results are not nearly as good. You can see from the table that the average percentage error is .676, much higher than the standard error of .286. The predicted values are all much too high. The 1961 prices for the first three châteaux in Table 6-5 are very high relative to the prices for the other years, which means that the ratios of the actual prices to the 1961 prices are very low. These ratios are not predicted to be this low, which leads to the large errors.

We are thus left with the conclusion that the theory does well if we take as actual prices the prices of the seconds crus châteaux but not if we include the premiers crus châteaux (and Cheval Blanc). Remember that we are trying to explain wine quality, and we are using wine prices to measure wine quality. If wine prices deviate more from wine quality for the top châteaux than for the others (for conspicuous consumption or Robert Parker reasons), then this argues for using the seconds crus châteaux only, which is good for the theory.

There is another test of the theory that could be done. There are 36 bottles of wine represented in Table 6-5. Take these bottles and do a blind taste test using, say, 20 wine experts (Robert Parker could be included). Each expert could rate each wine from, say, 1 to 10, and from these data we could create a quality index for each of the six vintages. The value of the index for a vintage would be its actual value, and the actual values could be compared to the predicted values as is done in Table 6-6. The theory could then be judged by how well the actual values were predicted. This comparison would have the advantage of eliminating any conspicuous consumption effects. (Another possibility to lessen the number of wines to be sampled would be to pour the six châteaux's wines for each vintage year into a large pitcher and to have the experts just sample each pitcher. I have been told that this is not a good idea.)

The taste test would eliminate the problem of finding representative prices for the wines. If you, say, search for wine prices on the Internet, you will find that the same wine (same chateau and year) has a fairly wide range of prices. The wine prices in Table 6-5 have the advantage of all being chosen by the same store, but there is no guarantee that each price in the table is representative of prices of the wine elsewhere.

You might ask if this comparison using quality indices would be a good test of the theory since the theory was estimated using prices, not quality indices. The comparison would be a good test provided that the prices from 1980 back, which were used in the estimation, were not influenced by conspicuous consumption effects and thus reflected the true quality of the wine. In other words, if the problem of prices not reflecting quality is a phenomenon that began after 1980, the coefficients in Box 6-2 are legitimate to use in a test using quality indices.

Can One Make Money?

Once the weather is known for a vintage (at the end of September of the vintage year), a prediction of the vintage price can be made using the coefficients in Box 6-2. This is a prediction based on the actual values of the weather variables, but it is not a prediction that can be immediately compared to the actual vintage price because the actual price is unknown. A number of years have to pass before the actual quality of the vintage is known and thus the actual price is known.

Since there are large auction markets for wine, including recently bottled wines, it is possible that one could make money buying or selling cases. If, for example, our prediction for the price of the current vintage is very high (because the three weather variables are favorable) and if the current auction price of the wine is much lower than this, one could make money by buying the wine now and selling it later (after the true quality of the wine becomes known and the price rises). If, on the other hand, our prediction is for a low price and the current auction price is higher, we should sell the wine now (if this is possible) and buy it back later. (If there are now conspicuous consumption effects for the top châteaux, it would be best to avoid these châteaux and concentrate on, say, the seconds crus.)

In other words, if you know something the auction market does not, you may be able to take advantage of it. In general, however, markets work fairly well, and possibly, the weather information has already been adequately incorporated into the current price. It may even be that some market participants are using the coefficients in Box 6-2 to make predictions! But then again, if most participants are like the authors of *The Wine Spectator*, there may be money to be made.

7 College Grades and Class Attendance

The student's life is pleasant,
    And pleasant is his labour,
Search all Ireland over
    You'll find no better neighbour.

Nor lords nor petty princes
    Dispute the student's pleasure,
Nor chapter stints his purse
    Nor stewardship his leisure.

None orders early rising,
    Calf-rearing or cow-tending,
Nor nights of toilsome vigil,
    His time is his for spending.

He takes a hand at draughts,
    And plucks a harp-string bravely,
And fills his nights with courting
    Some golden-haired light lady.

And when spring-time is come,
    The ploughshaft's there to follow,
A fistful of goosequills,
    And a straight deep furrow!
        Frank O'Connor, The Student

Much to the chagrin of both parents and teachers, many college students skip classes. Does skipping classes have any effect on a student's grade in the class? If it does, by how much? We will see in this chapter that grades do suffer if more than four classes are skipped in a semester, so there is some cost to students who skip many classes. I begin my courses by pointing out this result in the hope that students will see the light and stop any planned skipping behavior.

Although the focus of this chapter is on class attendance, the results are of more general interest. The basic question is what determines a student's grade in a class, and we will see that there are many variables that matter. This chapter is based on an article by Garey C. Durden and Larry V. Ellis, "The Effects of Attendance on Student Learning in Principles of Economics," *American Economic Review* (May 1995): 343–346.

Theory and Data

The variable to be explained is a student's grade in a principles of economics course in a midsize college in North Carolina. The grade is in percentage terms from 0 to 100 percent. Students were sampled over three semesters—spring and fall 1993 and spring 1994. The number of students sampled was 346. The data from those surveys are listed in Table 7-1.

The first variable in Table 7-1 is the dependent variable—grade. As just noted, it is in percentage terms. This is the grade in the principles of economics course.

A typical procedure in a study like this is to include as many explanatory variables in the analysis as seem theoretically plausible. Theory is used to exclude unlikely variables, so the variables that remain have a ring of plausibility to them. Then the best fitting set of coefficients is found using all the theoretically plausible variables, and the t-statistics are computed and examined. Explanatory variables with t-statistics greater than about 2.0 or less than about –2.0 are taken to be significant, and the rest are not. Variables that are not significant are usually dropped from the analysis. The variables in Table 7-1 are meant to be plausible theoretical candidates for explaining the course grade. We will see in the next section how many are significant.

Let's go through the variables in Table 7-1 one by one. There are five variables that measure absences from class: skip12, skip34, skip45, skip67, and skip8+. For example, skip12 has a value of 1 if the student has skipped only 1 or 2 classes and has a value of 0 otherwise. Using these five variables allows us to see how many classes can be skipped (if any) without having the course grade suffer.

SATmath is the student's SAT math score, and SATverbal is the student's SAT verbal score. To the extent that SAT scores measure academic

TABLE **7-1**   Data for testing the theory that class attendance affects grades

Variable	Description	Mean
grade	Student course grade	72.234
skip12	1 if 1 or 2 absences; 0 otherwise	0.277
skip34	1 if 3 or 4 absences; 0 otherwise	0.159
skip56	1 if 5 or 6 absences; 0 otherwise	0.162
skip78	1 if 7 or 8 absences; 0 otherwise	0.061
skip9+	1 if 9 or more absences; 0 otherwise	0.104
SATmath	Math SAT score	515.647
SATverbal	Verbal SAT score	466.960
GPA	Grade point average (4-point scale times 100)	269.538
colprep	1 if high school program was college prep; 0 otherwise	.538
HSecon	1 if had high school economics; 0 otherwise	.454
calculus	1 if have taken college calculus; 0 otherwise	.532
econ	1 if previously had a college economics course; 0 otherwise	.419
hoursstudy	Number of hours per week studying economics	2.400
hourswork	Number of hours worked per week in a job	7.818
credithours	Number of credit hours carried during current semester	13.081
extracurr	1 if one or more extracurricular activities; 0 otherwise	.720
fratsor	1 if fraternity or sorority member; 0 otherwise	.214
parents	0 if either of the student's parents had a high school education or less; 1 if either parent had some college; 2 if either parent had a college degree; and 3 if either parent studied at the graduate level	1.621
white	1 if white; 0 otherwise	.951
male	1 if male; 0 if female	.621
local	1 if from North Carolina; 0 otherwise	.899

ability, they should have a positive effect on the course grade; high ability students should do better, other things being equal, than low ability ones. A measure of both ability and motivation is the student's overall grade point average (GPA) before enrolling in the course. We would expect the GPA variable to have a positive effect on the course grade.

The next four variables pertain to the student's high school and college preparation. The colprep variable is 1 if the student's high school program was college prep and is 0 otherwise. The HSecon variable is 1 if the student had high school economics and is 0 otherwise. The calculus variable is 1 if the student has had college calculus and is 0 otherwise.

The econ variable is 1 if the student previously had a college economics course and is 0 otherwise. We would expect these four variables to have a positive effect on the course grade.

The next five variables concern how the student spends his or her time in college. The hoursstudy variable is the number of hours per week spent studying economics, the hourswork variable is the number of hours worked per week in a job, and the credithours variable is the number of credit hours carried during the current semester. The extracurr variable is 1 if the student has one or more extracurricular activities and is 0 otherwise, and the fratsor variable is 1 if the student belongs to a fraternity or sorority and 0 otherwise. We would expect hoursstudy to have a positive effect on the course grade and the other four to have a negative effect.

The parents variable is meant to pick up family background effects. It is a measure of the amount of schooling the student's parents have had. The male variable is 1 if the student is male and 0 if female. The white variable is 1 if the student is white and 0 otherwise. Finally, the local variable is 1 if the student is from North Carolina (the home state) and 0 if not.

To summarize, the 21 variables in Table 7-1 after grade, which is the dependent variable, are possible variables that affect the student's course grade. The theory is that these variables may matter in terms of affecting how well the student does in the course. We will see in the next section which ones seem to matter and which do not.

Fit and Test and Examine the Results

There are 22 coefficients to estimate: the coefficient for each of the explanatory variables in Table 7-1 plus the intercept. The best fitting set of coefficients was found in the usual way, and then the t-statistics were computed. The results are shown in Box 7-1.

Let's get right to the main point. Does class attendance matter? You can see that skip12 and skip34 are not significant, but skip56 and skip 9+ are, and skip78 nearly is (t-statistic of -1.83). The results thus say that if you skip 5 or more classes, your grade will suffer. For example, the coefficient for skip56 is -3.228, which says that with 5 or 6 absences the grade falls 3.228 percentage points. So it does not matter for the first

BOX **7-1**

grade depends on:		t-statistic
0.465	skip12	0.38
−1.538	skip34	−1.11
−3.228	skip56	−2.29
−3.475	skip78	−1.83
−3.521	skip9+	2.12
0.011	SATmath	1.97
0.014	SATverbal	2.35
0.078	GPA	9.13
−0.097	colprep	0.11
2.766	HSecon	3.35
3.352	calculus	3.75
−1.027	econ	1.19
0.093	hoursstudy	0.41
−0.049	hourswork	1.28
−0.021	credithours	0.27
−0.595	extracurr	0.60
−1.886	fratsor	1.80
0.695	parents	1.83
4.524	white	2.33
0.736	male	0.80
−0.737	local	−0.54
33.919	intercept	3.94
number of observations: 346		

4 absences (because skip12 and skip34 have small t-statistics and are thus not significant), but after that it does. This result, of course, seems sensible. Missing a few classes is probably not a big deal, but there is a limit.

What about the other variables? The three variables measuring ability matter. SATmath has a t-statistic of 1.97, which is essentially 2.0, and SATverbal has a t-statistic of 2.35. The GPA variable has a huge

t-statistic (9.13) and is thus significant. Not surprisingly, how a student has done in previous courses is significant in explaining how the student will do in the principles of economics course.

The HSecon variable is significant (t-statistic of 3.35), and the calculus variable is significant (t-statistic of 3.75). It thus matters whether the student has had economics in high school and whether he or she has had calculus. The estimated effects are fairly large. The coefficient for calculus is 3.352, and so calculus adds 3.352 percentage points to the course grade, other things being equal. The coefficient for HSecon is 2.766.

There is only one other variable in Box 7-1 that is significant, which is the white variable. The coefficient is 4.524 and the t-statistic is 2.33. This says that, other things being equal, white students score 4.524 percentage points higher than nonwhite students. It is unclear what is going on here. Only 4.9 percent of the students in the sample are nonwhite, and this result may be a fluke in the sense that the large coefficient is heavily influenced by a few very low nonwhite scores. If the result is not a fluke, it says there is something in the background of nonwhite students not captured by the other explanatory variables that has a negative effect on the course grade.

Two other variables are close to being significant: parents with a t-statistic of 1.83 and fratsor with a t-statistic of -1.80. Both may thus play a role. The coefficient for fratsor is -1.89, which means that being a Greek, other things being equal, lowers your score by 1.89 percentage points.

All the remaining variables have t-statistics that lead to their rejection as explanatory variables. These are colprep, hoursstudy, hourswork, credithours, extracurr, male, and local. Since these variables are rejected, one could reestimate the coefficients with these variables excluded. Box 7-1 would then have seven fewer coefficients. The authors of the study did not do this in their article, and so I cannot present it here.

If these results are to be trusted (we discuss possible pitfalls in the next section), they may be of use to college administrators. One possibility, for example, would be to require calculus because calculus is quite significant. Another possibility would be to take attendance to discourage students from skipping more than about 4 classes. For large lecture courses, I have suggested putting chips in shoes, as is done in road races, where the chips would be recorded as the students entered the lecture hall. This suggestion has not been received with open arms, but the technology is still new to some people.

Possible Pitfalls

These results are based on a survey of students in one type of course (principles of economics) in one type of college (midsize, in North Carolina). Perhaps the effects are different in different courses and colleges, so generalizing these results to other courses and colleges is somewhat risky. In particular, some of the rejected variables could be significant in other studies.

It is important to realize what we mean by the effects possibly being different in other courses and colleges. We know from Chapter 5 that a sample need not be a random draw from a population for the results to be valid. In the case of the extramarital affairs data, the sample does not have to be a random draw from the population as long as the selection criterion does not depend on the size of the dependent variable. When we say this, however, we are assuming that the coefficients are the same for everyone. As we discussed in Chapter 5, people can differ in the values of the explanatory variables but not in the coefficients that are attached to these variables. If coefficients differ across groups of individuals, we must treat each group separately in the sense of finding the best fitting set of coefficients group by group.

For the present example, we are thus saying that the coefficients that pertain to students in the principles of economics course in a midsize college in North Carolina may not be the same as the coefficients in other courses and colleges. If this is so, then the results in Box 7-1 cannot be generalized.

Another possible pitfall is that some students may have filled out the survey incorrectly. If there are errors in measuring the explanatory variables, the coefficient estimates for these variables will in general be incorrect (biased). For example, it is a little odd that the hoursstudy variable is not significant in Box 7-1, and perhaps students did not do a good job estimating their study hours in the survey.

Predict

If we exclude the insignificant variables in Box 7-1, we know at the beginning of the semester everything we need to know about the student except the skip variables. By making assumptions about the skip variables for a given student, we can thus predict his or her course grade. Say that under the assumption that the student skips no classes, the predicted course grade is 81.000 percent, a B–. Now say the student is planning to skip 5 classes. The predicted value is now 81.000 minus 3.228 (the coefficient for skip56), which is 77.772, a C+. We would thus advise the student that skipping the 5 classes could lower the grade from a B– to a C+.

As a final word of warning, remember that there are errors attached to any prediction. We have not discussed the size of the standard error in this chapter. The article upon which this chapter is based did not in fact present the standard error. Its main concern was whether the skip variables were significant and what the sizes of their coefficients were. There is, however, undoubtedly a nontrivial standard error, so any prediction has uncertainty attached to it.

8   Marathon Times

If you can fill the unforgiving minute
   With sixty seconds' worth of distance run,
Yours is the Earth and everything that's in it,
   And—which is more—you'll be a Man, my son!
      Rudyard Kipling, from If—

Do not go gentle into that good night,
Old age should burn and rave at close of day;
Rage, rage against the dying of the light.
      Dylan Thomas, from Do Not Go Gentle into That Good Night

This chapter, my favorite, is concerned with a particular physical activity, namely, running marathons. Although most readers of this book probably have never run a marathon (if they have, I am probably not selling many books!), it is never too late to start. Marathon running is life writ small. With its work, strategy, pain, and pleasure of pushing oneself to the limits, disappointment at doing poorly, joy of doing well, and alas, the inevitable slowing down with age, it mimics much of what life is about.

The question considered in this chapter is how marathon times change with age. If you ran a marathon in 3 hours at age 35, what can you expect to do at age 50 or at age 70? We want to estimate the rate at which people slow down with age.

Although the focus in this chapter is on marathon times, the analysis has broader implications. The broader question concerns the rate at which people physically decline with age. How much, for example, can be physically expected of a healthy, noninjured 75-year-old man or woman relative to what he or she could do at age 45? If we can get good estimates of how fast people physically decline, we can use these estimates to think about social policies on aging. Policies on aging should obviously depend on the decline rate. If, for example, the rate remains small into fairly old age, then policies designed to keep people physically fit will have more payoff than if the rate increases rapidly with age. The size of the rate is also relevant for retirement policies. The smaller the rate, the less emphasis should probably be placed on plans to have people retire earlier than they would otherwise want to. The size of the rate may also be relevant for the question of how wage rates should change with age.

A Theory of the Decline Rate

It is obvious that people slow down with age. No one expects a world-class 60-year-old marathoner to be competitive with a world-class 30-year-old marathoner. However, we would like to know more than this. We would like to know what the decline rate is at different ages. What is the decline rate at age 50, at age 60, at age 70, and so on? The theory that we are going to use is depicted in Figure 8-1. The time taken for a task is on the vertical axis, and age is on the horizontal axis. The vertical axis is in percentage terms, which means that equal distances on the vertical axis are equal percentage changes. For example, the distance on the vertical axis from 10 to 15, an increase of 50 percent, is the same as the distance on the vertical axis from 100 to 150, also an increase of 50 percent. We are using the percentage scale because we want to base the theory in percentage terms. "Decline rate" in this chapter means percentage decline.

The line in Figure 8-1 shows that between age 35 and some transition age, the percentage increase in the time taken for the task is the same from year to year. For example, if at age 41 the decline rate is 1.0 percent, it is also 1.0 percent at age 42. Prior to the transition age, we decline each year, but the *size* of the decline rate does not change.

At the transition age, the line starts to curve upward, which means that the decline rate begins to increase. For example, if at age 78 the decline rate were 1.6 percent, it would be larger at age 79, such as 1.9 percent. The curve reflects the idea that at some age things begin to get worse faster. The curve in Figure 8-1 is a "quadratic." The quadratic curve has the feature that the *increase* in the decline rate is the same from age to age. For example, if from age 78 to 79 the decline rate increases by 0.3 percentage points from 1.6 percent to 1.9 percent, then from age 80 to 81 it

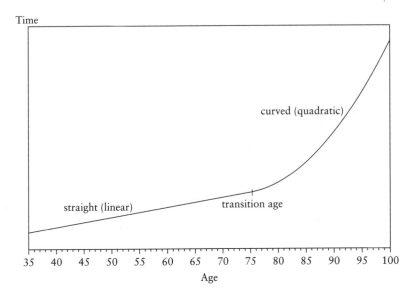

FIGURE **8-1**   Time taken for a task by age

will increase from 1.9 percent to 2.2 percent. The 0.3 increase is the same from age to age.

The main idea behind Figure 8-1 is simple. It is that at least by age 35 people begin to slow down and that at some age the decline rate begins to increase. The two specific assumptions in the figure are (1) the decline rate does not change between age 35 and some transition age and (2) the *increase* in the decline rate after the transition rate is the same from age to age.

Although the main idea behind Figure 8-1 is obvious, what is not so obvious is how we determine the line. The three things to determine are (1) the decline rate before the transition age, (2) the transition age, and (3) the amount by which the decline rate increases from year to year after the transition age. The data that are used for this purpose are discussed next.

The Data

What data might we use to determine the line in Figure 8-1? Since we are focusing on the marathon, one possibility is to take an individual who ran a marathon every year and use his or her times to fit the line. The problem with this is that any one runner has good years and bad years depending on motivation, injury, weather during the race, and so on, so we may not be sampling a person's best effort each year.

Another possibility is to take a large race like the New York City marathon or the Boston marathon and compute the average time for each age. We could compute the average time for all 35-year-olds, for all 36-year-olds, and so on. We could then plot these average times to see how the average times change with age. This is a really bad idea. It suffers from huge selection issues. As runners age, many quit running marathons. Many people run marathons in their 30s and 40s and then decide they have had enough. What kind of people are left who run marathons in, say, their 70s? Generally, they are better than average runners. People who are not very good at running marathons tend to drop out more than do those who are good. The average quality of a 70-year-old runner in the New York City marathon relative to all 70-year-olds is much higher than the average quality of a 35-year-old runner relative to all 35-year-olds. So looking at average times across ages is very misleading. It includes the effects of aging and the effects of less talented runners retiring earlier from marathon running. In fact, sometimes when these age averages are computed for a given race, the average time for, say, 65-year-olds is lower than the average time for, say, 40-year-olds!

Selection problems like this pervade many areas of statistics. They are easy to see in the case of running, but not so obvious in other disciplines. They are very common in medical studies. Suppose one had a truly random sample of 90-year-olds and a truly random sample of 70-year-olds. Say from these two samples, characteristics like blood pressure and bone density were measured. Very possibly, average blood pressure is lower in the 90-year-olds than in the 70-year-olds, and average bone density is higher. This does not mean, however, that blood pressure declines with age and bone density increases. It just means that people who make it to 90 are on average better physical specimens than those who die between 70 and 90.

Back to our estimation problem. We have so far rejected using only one individual and using average times by age. We will do the following instead. We will consider each point on the line in Figure 8-1 to be the biological minimum for that age across all humans, the fastest time that the best human of that age could run. We have, fortunately, an observation of this time, which is the best time for that age. Table 8-1 presents the best records by age as of the end of 2003 for U.S. citizens. The only systematic data available were for U.S. citizens. The one exception in Table 8-1 is Fauja Singh, who is a U.K. citizen. The times in the table increase from 2:11:40 (2 hours, 11 minutes, 40 seconds) for age 35 to 5:40:04 for age 92. We will use the data in Table 8-1 to determine the line in Figure 8-1. This will allow us to determine the decline rate, the transition age, and the increase in the decline rate after the transition age.

Before we fit the data, however, we need to pause to consider whether what we are doing is sensible. Where might we go wrong? We

TABLE **8-1**   Best marathon times by age (nondominated times)

Age	Time	Record Holder	Race	Race Date
35	2:11:40	Rod Dehaven	LaSalle Banks Chicago	10/07/01
42	2:12:47	Eddy Hellebuyck	Twin Cities	10/05/03
43	2:22:48	Jim Bowers	Humboldt Redwoods	10/10/82
44	2:22:55	Doug Kurtis	WZYP Rocket City	12/14/96
45	2:25:50	Jim Bowers	Humboldt Redwoods	10/14/84
52	2:25:51	Norm Green	Wigal Champ	12/02/84
53	2:31:20	Norm Green	Marine Corps	11/03/85
54	2:32:28	Norm Green	Lincoln	05/03/87
55	2:33:49	Norm Green	Lincoln	05/01/88
58	2:37:40	Alex Ratelle	Nike OTC	09/12/82
	&	Norm Green	Twin Cities	10/14/90
64	2:42:44	Clive Davies	Portland	10/28/79
66	2:42:49	Clive Davies	Nike OTC	09/13/81
68	2:52:45	Clive Davies	Lincoln	05/06/84
69	3:00:57	Monty Montgomery	Western Hemisphere	12/07/75
71	3:00:58	John Keston	Twin Cities	10/06/96
72	3:09:10	Warren Utes	Twin Cities	10/04/92
73	3:12:44	Warren Utes	Twin Cities	10/03/93
75	3:18:10	Warren Utes	LaSalle Banks Chicago	10/15/95
76	3:22:59	John Keston	Portland	09/30/01
77	3:33:27	Ed Benham	Wigal Champ	12/02/84
78	3:36:59	Warren Utes	Twin Cities	10/04/98
79	3:49:23	Ed Benham	Calloway Gardens	01/10/87
80	4:13:12	Lloyd Young	Twin Cities	10/05/03
84	4:17:51	Ed Benham	Twin Cities	10/06/91
85	5:11:04	Henry Sypniewski	Erie	09/14/03
92	5:40:04	Fauja Singh	Toronto	09/23/03

don't have the problem of one individual having good years and bad years because we are using many individuals—the best one at each age. Also, we don't have the problem of less talented individuals quitting earlier because we are just using the best one at each age. The most serious problem we probably face is that some of the record times may not be close to the biological minimum. Although hundreds of thousands of people of many ages have run marathons, there is no guarantee that the best time so far for a given age is the biological minimum. This is especially true for the older ages. For example, the record for age 84 in Table 8-1 may not be close to the best that could ever be done. Think about it this way. In the next 20 years, if hundreds of thousands of people age 84 run a marathon, the time of 4:17:51 in Table 8-1 could be lowered considerably. This potential problem will be called a "small sample" problem. The sample for a given age may not be large enough to get a good estimate of the biological minimum.

We have attempted to mitigate the effects of the small sample problem by excluding any age time that was slower than a time for an older age. For example, there is no age 46 in Table 8-1 because the time for this age, 2:26:21, is slower than the age 52 time of 2:25:51. Since we don't expect times to decrease with age, any age for which the time is slower than the time for an older age must suffer from the small sample problem. Since we know that the biological minimum for age 52 is at least 2:25:51, the biological minimum for age 46 must be lower than this. We would expect the age 46 time to come down considerably in the future as we get a larger sample of 46-year-olds running marathons.

A good example of the excluding of dominated times concerns Norm Green, who you can see from the table holds the record for ages 52, 53, 54, 55, and 58. Green also holds the record for age 51, but his time at age 51 was 2:29:11, which is slower than his time at age 52 of 2:25:51. Green's age 51 time is not included in the table. As good as his time was at age 51, it was obviously not his biological minimum. Green ran his first marathon at age 49, and so he may have still been learning at age 51.

We also did not use the age 35 observation in Table 8-1 in the estimation. The time is 2:11:40, which is only slightly lower than the age 42 time of 2:12:47. It seems unlikely that in 7 years the biological minimum time would increase by only 1 minute and 7 seconds. In other words, given that someone age 42 ran a 2:12:47 marathon, the time of 2:11:40

for age 35 seems too high. It may not be a good estimate of the biological minimum time for age 35, and so we have not used it. More on this later.

You might ask, what if all ages are getting faster over time because of things like better nutrition, better training methods, better shoes, and so on? Fortunately, this problem is not serious as long as all ages are getting better at the same rate. All this would do is shift the line down in Figure 8-1. It would not affect the decline rate, the transition age, or the increase in the decline rate after the transition age. Progress would only be a problem if it affects the various ages differently. This also means that using only U.S. citizens and using only data through 2003 for the estimation are not as limiting as you might at first think. If adding more countries and more recent data affect all ages similarly, the coefficients should not be changed much except for the intercept. Because all ages may improve in the future, our use of the phrase "biological minimum" is not quite right. To be precise, we should put "almost" in front of it.

Fit and Examine and Possible Pitfalls

Now comes the fun part, which is to find the line that best fits the times in Table 8-1. The line in Figure 8-1 is determined by four coefficients: the intercept, the slope up to the transition age, the transition age, and the increase in the slope after the transition age. You can think about a computer trying thousands of lines like that in the figure (that is, thousands of sets of four coefficients) and choosing the line that provides the smallest sum of squared errors. This would be the best fitting line.

In the present case, however, there is a restriction we want to impose. We would like none of the actual times to be below the line. If the line is to reflect the biological minimum at each age, it would not make sense to have any time below the minimum. This restriction is imposed by simply having the computer try only lines that lie below all the times. The error for each age is the distance from the time to the line, and the restriction forces all the errors to be nonnegative. The computer computes all the errors, squares them, and then adds them up. Each line thus has a sum of squared errors associated with it, and the computer finds the one with the smallest sum.

We have imposed one other restriction on the estimation. This study of marathon times is part of a larger study of the effects of aging in sports. Other running events have been analyzed as well as field events, swimming events, and chess. It turns out that decline rates are similar across a number of events. In the case of the marathon, similar decline rates are found for 800-, 1,500-, 5,000-, and 10,000-meter track events and 5- and 10-kilometer road racing events. In the estimation, we have imposed the restriction that for these six events and the marathon, the decline rate, the transition age, and the change in the decline rate are the same. In other words, the line in Figure 8-1 is the same for all seven events except for the intercept, which is obviously different for each event. The fitting procedure is to find the decline rate, the transition age, the change in the decline rate, and the seven intercepts that give the best fit subject to the restriction that no actual time for a given age and event is smaller than the predicted time.

An advantage of pooling the seven events as we have done is that more observations are used to estimate the decline rate, the transition age, and the change in the decline rate. A disadvantage is the assumption that these three coefficients being the same across the seven events may not be true. There is thus a trade-off between having more observations and having the estimates depend on a possibly bad assumption. We have chosen to make the assumption, and this is a potential pitfall to keep in mind.

The line that gave the best fit is shown in Figure 8-2, which uses the estimated intercept for the marathon. You can see that the transition age is 75.1 years. Before this age, the decline rate is constant at 0.80 percent per year. After age 75.1, the decline rate increases each year, and the amount of the increase is 0.328 per year. Three of the four coefficients are thus 75.1 for the transition age, 0.80 for the decline rate before the transition age, and 0.328 for the increase in the decline rate after the transition age. The estimated intercept for the marathon determines the vertical position of the line. The line crosses the age 35 axis at a time of 2:06:07.

We are not reporting t-statistics because their use is not the best way to think about testing the theory. It is obvious that none of the coefficients are zero. For example, no one would think that the decline rate is zero or that after some age the decline rate does not begin to increase. The procedure used here is to fit the line and then examine what the fitted line implies.

First, note from Figure 8-2 that the age 35 predicted time of 2:06:07 is considerably below the record time of 2:11:40. Remember that

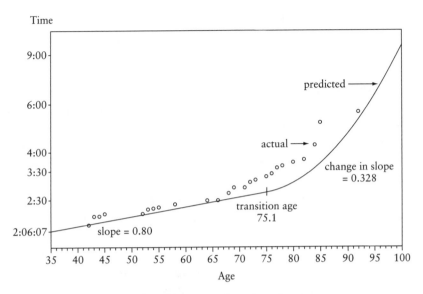

FIGURE **8-2**   Actual and predicted best marathon times by age

we did not use the age 35 time of 2:11:40 in the estimation. Is the 2:06:07 predicted time unrealistically low? It turns out no. The world record time at the time of this writing (November 2010) belongs to Haile Gebrselassie of Ethiopia, who on September 28, 2008, at the age of 35, ran a 2:03:59 marathon in Berlin. So the age 35 predicted time is slower than the current record time. This is an example where adding non-U.S. citizens and data since 2003 would lower the record times in Table 8-1. Again, if this affects all ages similarly, it will have modest effects on the estimated line in Figure 8-2 except for the intercept.

An interesting feature of Figure 8-2 is that after age 66 and before age 92 the actual times are noticeably above the estimated line. This analysis thus suggests that the records for these ages are soft. You might ask why such a long string of observations is noticeably above the line. For example, the fit looks like it would be better if the estimated transition age were closer to 66 than 75, with the quadratic part of the line then being closer to the actual times (but still hitting the age 92 time). The answer is the pooling. The decline rate, the transition age, and the change in the decline rate are determined using observations from all seven events. The use of observations from all seven events results in the shape of the line in Figure 8-2. This is not exactly the shape that would result if only the marathon observations were used.

One of the other six events is 800 meters, and Figure 8-3 shows the actual observations for this event along with the fitted line. This figure uses the estimated intercept for 800 meters. Otherwise, the line is the same as in Figure 8-2. You can see first that there are more observations for 800 meters than for the marathon and second that the 800-meter observations are in general closer to the line.

Figures 8-2 and 8-3 show clearly the issue involved in pooling the events. Do we trust the marathon times enough to use only these times in estimating the line, or do we use information in observations for other events to help determine the line? There are potential pitfalls in either case, which need to be kept in mind. As more and better observations become available, if the marathon record times come close to the line based on pooling, this is evidence in favor of the pooling assumption. If not, this will suggest treating the marathon separately.

Table 8-2 gives more detail regarding the results in Figure 8-2. This table is the same as Table 8-1 except that the points on the line are presented along with the deviations of the actual times from the line.

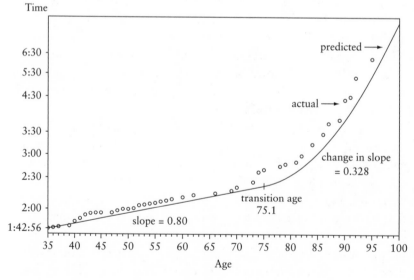

FIGURE **8-3**   Actual and predicted best 800-meter times by age

TABLE **8-2** Best and potential marathon times by age (nondominated times)

Age	Actual Time	Potential Time	Actual Minus Potential	Record Holder	Race	Race Date
35	2:11:40	2:06:07	5:33	Rod Dehaven	LaSalle Banks Chicago	10/07/01
42	2:12:47	2:13:24	−0:37	Eddy Hellebuyck	Twin Cities	10/05/03
43	2:22:48	2:14:29	8:19	Jim Bowers	Humboldt Redwoods	10/10/82
44	2:22:55	2:15:34	7:21	Doug Kurtis	WZYP Rocket City	12/14/96
45	2:25:50	2:16:39	9:11	Jim Bowers	Humboldt Redwoods	10/14/84
52	2:25:51	2:24:33	1:18	Norm Green	Wigal Champ	12/02/84
53	2:31:20	2:25:43	5:37	Norm Green	Marine Corps	11/03/85
54	2:32:28	2:26:53	5:35	Norm Green	Lincoln	05/03/87
55	2:33:49	2:28:04	5:45	Norm Green	Lincoln	05/01/88
58	2:37:40	2:31:41	5:59	Alex Ratelle	Nike OTC	09/12/82
			&	Norm Green	Twin Cities	10/14/90
64	2:42:44	2:39:10	3:34	Clive Davies	Portland	10/28/79
66	2:42:49	2:41:45	1:04	Clive Davies	Nike OTC	09/13/81
68	2:52:45	2:44:22	8:23	Clive Davies	Lincoln	05/06/84
69	3:00:57	2:45:41	15:16	Monty Montgomery	Western Hemisphere	12/07/75
71	3:00:58	2:48:22	12:36	John Keston	Twin Cities	10/06/96
72	3:09:10	2:49:43	19:27	Warren Utes	Twin Cities	10/04/92
73	3:12:44	2:51:05	21:39	Warren Utes	Twin Cities	10/03/93
75	3:18:10	2:53:52	24:18	Warren Utes	LaSalle Banks Chicago	10/15/95
76	3:22:59	2:55:31	27:28	John Keston	Portland	09/30/01
77	3:33:27	2:57:46	35:41	Ed Benham	Wigal Champ	12/02/84
78	3:36:59	3:00:38	36:21	Warren Utes	Twin Cities	10/04/98
79	3:49:23	3:04:09	45:14	Ed Benham	Calloway Gardens	01/10/87
80	4:13:12	3:08:22	1:04:50	Lloyd Young	Twin Cities	10/05/03
84	4:17:51	3:33:03	44:48	Ed Benham	Twin Cities	10/06/91
85	5:11:04	3:41:32	1:29:32	Henry Sypniewski	Erie	09/14/03
92	5:40:04	5:19:06	20:58	Fauja Singh	Toronto	09/23/03

The point on the line for a given age will be called the "potential" time. (Remember, however, that "potential" is really "almost potential.") The deviation from a time to the line is the difference between the actual time and the potential time. This deviation for a given age is the "error" for that age.

The smallest errors in Table 8-2 are for ages 42, 52, and 66. After 66, as is evident from Figure 8-2, the errors get larger. The error for age 92 is small relative to errors for ages in the late 70s and the 80s. The error for age 42 is close to zero but negative. The estimation restriction discussed earlier does not exactly force every error to be nonnegative as this result shows. The error is, however, quite small. Overall, Table 8-2 suggests that many marathon age records are likely to fall over time.

Table 8-2 contains only the times that were used in the estimation—the nondominated times. Although dominated times were not used, once the line is determined, it can be used to predict times for all ages, not just the ages in Table 8-2. The predicted (potential) time for a given age is just the point on the line for that age. Table 8-3 presents the actual and potential times for these other ages. As expected, the potential time for each of these ages is less than the actual time and, in many cases, by a large amount. According to this analysis, the dominated times are, of course, softer than the nondominated times, which should lead to large record changes in the future for the dominated times.

Back to possible pitfalls, this analysis is probably most vulnerable for the oldest ages, where there are fewer observations. For example, looking at Figure 8-2, perhaps the potential times for ages between about 70 and 90 are too low. If so, then for these ages, the actual minus potential times in Tables 8-2 and 8-3 are too large; the records for these ages are not as soft as the tables suggest. For example, it may not be sensible to assume that the increase in the decline rate remains constant after age 85 or so. Maybe there should be a second transition age after which the decline rate increases by larger amounts each year. In other words, the quadratic curve might be a good approximation between about ages 75 and 85, and then after 85, a steeper curve might be needed. We don't yet have enough observations at the oldest ages to be able to say much.

Now back to Table 8-3. If we take the line all the way out to age 100, we get a potential time of 9:49:42. There are no records beyond age 92, so we have no idea whether this is too optimistic or too pessimistic.

TABLE **8-3** Best and potential marathon times by age (dominated times)

Age	Actual Time	Potential Time	Actual Minus Potential	Record Holder	Race	Race Date
36	2:15:35	2:07:08	8:27	Don Janicki	Revco-Cleveland	05/05/96
37	2:12:51	2:08:09	4:42	Steve Plasencia	Twin Cities	10/02/94
38	2:17:26	2:09:11	8:15	Budd Coates	Olympic Trials: Charlotte	02/17/96
39	2:14:20	2:10:14	4:06	Steve Plasencia	Olympic Trials: Charlotte	02/17/96
40	2:17:02	2:11:17	5:45	Kenneth Judson	Rocket City	12/08/90
41	2:17:05	2:12:20	4:45	Paul Pilkington	LaSalle Banks Chicago	10/24/99
46	2:26:21	2:17:45	8:36	Jim Bowers	Humboldt Redwoods	10/13/85
47	2:26:43	2:18:52	7:51	Bob Schlau	Houston-Tenneco	01/15/95
48	2:30:45	2:19:59	10:46	Jim Knerr	Santa Monica	08/29/82
49	2:33:03	2:21:07	11:56	Ken Sparks	Detroit Free Press Int'l	10/16/94
50	2:34:21	2:22:15	12:06	Michael Heffernan	Twin Cities	10/14/90
51	2:29:11	2:23:24	5:47	Norm Green	Lincoln	05/06/84
56	2:38:55	2:29:16	9:39	Alex Ratelle	City of Lakes	10/19/80
57	2:38:07	2:30:28	7:39	Alex Ratelle	Madeline Island	09/12/81
59	2:48:25	2:32:54	15:31	Alex Ratelle	Omaha Waterfront	11/05/83
60	2:47:46	2:34:08	13:38	Clive Davies	Nike OTC	10/12/75
61	2:43:11	2:35:23	7:48	Gaylon Jorgensen	Twin Cities	10/14/90
62	2:47:15	2:36:38	10:37	Jim O'Neill	LaSalle Banks Chicago	10/22/00
63	2:48:04	2:37:54	10:10	Clive Davies	Track Capital	05/06/79
65	2:51:27	2:40:27	11:00	Clive Davies	Trails End	02/28/81
67	2:55:15	2:43:03	12:12	Clive Davies	Emerald City	03/27/83
70	3:01:14	2:48:22	12:52	Warren Utes	Old Style Chicago	10/28/90
74	3:37:07	2:52:28	44:39	Ed Benham	Marine Corps	11/01/81
81	4:32:13	3:13:18	1:18:55	Anthony Napoli	Nissan Buffalo	05/26/02
82	4:38:00	3:19:01	1:18:59	Dudley Healy	Twin Cities	10/06/96
83	5:20:08	3:25:35	1:54:33	Max Bayne	British American	12/16/84
86	5:40:10	3:51:06	1:49:04	Ivor Welch	Avenue of Giants	05/03/81
87	6:48:44	4:01:52	2:46:52	Ivor Welch	San Francisco	07/11/82
88	6:52:30	4:13:59	2:39:31	Abraham Weintraub	Flora London	04/26/98

TABLE **8-3**   Best and potential marathon times by age (dominated times) (*continued*)

Age	Actual Time	Potential Time	Actual Minus Potential	Record Holder	Race	Race Date
89	6:35:38	4:27:35	2:08:03	Sam Gadless	City of Los Angeles	03/03/96
90	7:25:12	4:42:49	2:42:23	Abraham Weintraub	New York City	11/05/00
91	7:37:41	4:59:55	2:37:46	Abraham Weintraub	Flora London	04/20/01
93	none	5:40:38				
94	none	6:04:48				
95	none	6:31:58				
96	none	7:02:33				
97	none	7:37:01				
98	none	8:15:55				
99	none	8:59:53				
100	none	9:49:42				

A 9:49:42 marathon is about 22 minutes a mile, a little less than 3 miles an hour for about 10 hours.

Use the Results

If we are willing to take the line in Figure 8-2 as being a good approximation, at least up to ages below 80, we can do some useful things with it. We can first compute what are called *age-graded factors* or *age factors*. These are presented in Table 8-4. The age factors are calculated as follows. We first compute the potential time for age 35, which from Table 8-2 you can see is 2:06:07. We then compute the potential time for age 36, which you can see from Table 8-3 is 2:07:08. The age factor for age 36 is the age 36 time divided by the age 35 time, which is 1.008. We then compute the potential time for age 37, and the age factor for age 37 is the age 37 time divided by the age 35 time, which is 1.016. We do this for all the ages through age 100. The age factor for age 100 is 4.676, which is the potential age 100 time of 9:49:42 divided by the potential age 35 time of 2:06:07.

We also present in Table 8-4 the percentage change in the potential time from one age to the next. Through age 75, this is just 0.80 percent,

TABLE **8-4**   Age-graded factors for the marathon

Age	Age-Graded Factor	Percentage Change in Potential Time	Age	Age-Graded Factor	Percentage Change in Potential Time
35	1.000	0.00	68	1.303	0.80
36	1.008	0.80	69	1.314	0.80
37	1.016	0.80	70	1.324	0.80
38	1.024	0.80	71	1.335	0.80
39	1.033	0.80	72	1.346	0.80
40	1.041	0.80	73	1.357	0.80
41	1.049	0.80	74	1.368	0.80
42	1.058	0.80	75	1.379	0.80
43	1.066	0.80	76	1.392	0.95
44	1.075	0.80	77	1.410	1.27
45	1.084	0.80	78	1.432	1.60
46	1.092	0.80	79	1.460	1.93
47	1.101	0.80	80	1.494	2.26
48	1.110	0.80	81	1.533	2.59
49	1.119	0.80	82	1.578	2.92
50	1.128	0.80	83	1.630	3.24
51	1.137	0.80	84	1.689	3.57
52	1.146	0.80	85	1.757	3.90
53	1.155	0.80	86	1.832	4.23
54	1.165	0.80	87	1.918	4.56
55	1.174	0.80	88	2.014	4.89
56	1.184	0.80	89	2.122	5.21
57	1.193	0.80	90	2.243	5.54
58	1.203	0.80	91	2.378	5.87
59	1.212	0.80	92	2.530	6.20
60	1.222	0.80	93	2.701	6.53
61	1.232	0.80	94	2.893	6.86
62	1.242	0.80	95	3.108	7.18
63	1.252	0.80	96	3.350	7.51
64	1.262	0.80	97	3.624	7.84
65	1.272	0.80	98	3.932	8.17
66	1.283	0.80	99	4.281	8.50
67	1.293	0.80	100	4.676	8.83

the slope of the line up to the transition age. After age 75, the percentage change increases each year by 0.328. For example, the percentage change between age 80 and age 81 is 2.59 percent, and the percentage change between age 81 and 82 is 2.92 percent. The difference between 2.92 and 2.59 is 0.33—actually, 0.328 before rounding. Life gets more difficult after about age 90. Between 90 and 91, the decline rate is 5.87 percent. Between 99 and 100 the decline rate is 8.83 percent. (Remember, however, that the results are less reliable at the oldest ages.)

People may differ in how they read Table 8-4, but I am struck by how small the decline rates are. The age factor for age 75, for example, is 1.379, only 37.9 percent more than for age 35. It is not until age 88 that the potential time is twice the potential age 35 time: an age 88 factor of 2.014. Given these numbers, it may be that societies have been too pessimistic about losses from aging for individuals who stay healthy and fit. Societies may have passed laws dealing with old people under incorrect assumptions.

If we leave society for now and turn to individuals, does Table 8-4 have anything to say about you and me? Remember that the age factors in the table are based on results using data from world-class athletes. Since most of us are not world-class athletes, what can we learn? Fortunately, one assumption is all you need to be able to use the table on a personal basis. This assumption is that we differ from a world-class athlete by a certain percentage, and this percentage does not change as we age. If at age 35 in peak condition I am slower than a world-class athlete of the same age by 50 percent, then the assumption is that at age 70 in peak condition I am also slower than a world-class athlete of the same age by 50 percent. In other words, my decline rate is assumed to be the same as that of world-class athletes; I am just starting from a higher base (that is, a slower time).

Given this assumption, you can use Table 8-4 on a personal basis. For example, my best marathon performance was a time of 2:58:45 in 1987 at the Philadelphia marathon. I was 45 at the time. In 1995 at age 53, I ran the Hartford marathon in 3:10:00. Which was the better age-corrected performance? If I divide my age 45 time by 1.084, the age 45 factor, I get 2:44:54. If I divide my age 53 time by 1.155, the age 53 factor, I get 2:44:30. These two times are very close, but my age 53 performance age corrected is 24 seconds faster. I did slightly better at age 53 according to these numbers.

The age factors can also be used to predict future times. What should I aim for if I run a marathon at age 70? The age factor for age 70 is 1.324, and my predicted age 35 time is, as above, 2:44:30. This time multiplied by 1.324 is 3:37:48. So if at age 70 I am in peak shape (as I was at age 53) and not injured, the line predicts I should be able to run a 3:37:48 marathon. You can use the age factors in Table 8-4 to compute your own predictions. I have been told by people that this table changed their lives. No longer did they have to fret about not being able to achieve personal bests anymore. They still had a shot at an age-corrected personal best by using the age factors in the table. It's fine to slow down as long as you don't slow down faster than predicted! As a rough rule of thumb, you can think of yourself as slowing down from age 35 at a rate of about 0.8 percent per year until about age 75. At age 80, the rate is about 2 percent, and at age 85, it is about 4 percent.

There are three other points. First, although record times do not exist for many physical activities, such as mowing the lawn with a hand mower, shoveling snow, bagging groceries, and the like, it may be that the decline rates for these activities do not differ greatly from the rates in Table 8-4. The table may be a useful guide to much of your physical life.

Second, although the results in this chapter are based on data only for men, they are probably a fairly good guide for women as well. It is hard to estimate a line like that in Figure 8-1 using records for women because the small sample problem is severe for women. For example, relatively few women in their 70s and 80s have run a marathon, and for many ages, it is unlikely we are getting times near the biological limit. Probably, the best we can do for now is to assume that the men's results pertain to women as well.

Finally, a common measure of aerobic capacity in physiology is VO_{2max}. (We will not discuss here how this is measured.) It is well known that VO_{2max} declines with age, but unfortunately, there is nothing in the physiological literature for VO_{2max} that is equivalent to Table 8-4. The VO_{2max} results that are available so far thus do not provide much of a check on the results using best records. An interesting question for future work, however, is whether VO_{2max} results can be used to help estimate decline rates, especially for the oldest ages.

Other Events

It was mentioned earlier that the analysis in this chapter is part of a larger study of the effects of aging in sports. (See the reference in the Chapter Notes.) The marathon was pooled with the 800-, 1,500-,

5,000-, and 10,000-meter track events and the 5- and 10-kilometer road racing events. Other events that have been analyzed are the 100-, 200-, and 400-meter track events, many swimming events for both men and women, the high jump, and chess. For the sprint events (100-, 200-, and 400-meter track), the rate of decline at the older ages is less than it is for the longer distances. For swimming, the rates of decline are generally larger for women than they are for men. Chess shows much less decline than any of the other events.

There is an option on my Web site for a user to enter his or her time for a particular event and his or her age when the event occurred. The program returns potential times for that person by age, from age 35 through age 100. This program uses age-graded factors. If the event is the marathon or one of the events pooled with the marathon, the age-graded factors are those in Table 8-4. If it is some other event, the estimated age-graded factors for that event are used. If, for example, you ran a 3-hour marathon when you were 40, the program will tell you what you should be capable of at any other age. The goal is to keep on one's potential line!

Conclusion

We have used our statistical tools—primarily just choosing a best fitting line subject to some restrictions—to estimate how we physically decline with age. As discussed in this chapter, these results may be of interest to policy makers in deciding how to treat the aging. But then again, it may be that the age factors in Table 8-4 are only of interest to old runners as they run ever more slowly into the sunset.

9 Aging and Baseball

The time you won your town the race
We chaired you through the market-place;
Man and boy stood cheering by,
And home we brought you shoulder-high.

To-day, the road all runners come,
Shoulder-high we bring you home,
And set you at your threshold down,
Townsman of a stiller town.

Smart lad, to slip betimes away
From fields where glory does not stay,
And early though the laurel grows
It withers quicker than the rose.

Eyes the shady night has shut
Cannot see the record cut,
And silence sounds no worse than cheers
After earth has stopped the ears:

Now you will not swell the rout
Of lads that wore their honours out,
Runners whom renown outran
And the name died before the man.

So set, before its echoes fade,
The fleet foot on the sill of shade,
And hold to the low lintel up
The still-defended challenge-cup.

And round that early-laurelled head
Will flock to gaze the strengthless dead,
And find unwithered on its curls
The garland briefer than a girl's.

       A. E. Housman, To an Athlete Dying Young

A Theory of Aging Effects in Baseball

We move from running to baseball. Even a casual observer of baseball would likely have the view that baseball players on average get better for a while and then begin to slow down. A 23-year-old is likely to improve as he gains more experience, but at some point, an aging body begins to take over. The theory that we use in this chapter is very simple; it is depicted in Figure 9-1. On the vertical axis is some measure of the player's performance for the year, and on the horizontal axis is the player's age. The curve shows an increasing level of performance up to some age, which we will call the *peak-performance* age, or just *peak age*, and then a decreasing level of performance. The aim of this chapter is to estimate this curve for major league baseball players.

The main idea behind Figure 9-1 is obvious, as was the main idea behind Figure 8-1 that runners slow down after some age. The basic theory that baseball players on average improve for a while and then slow down is not subject to doubt and thus does not really have to be

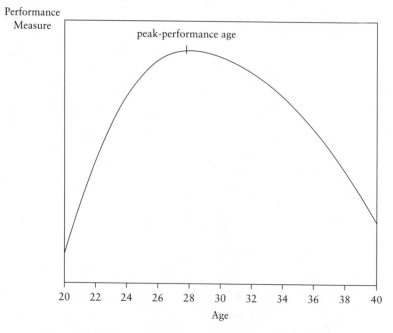

FIGURE **9-1**   Postulated relationship between performance and age

tested. What is not obvious is how to determine the shape of the curve in Figure 9-1.

One problem in determining the shape of the curve is that players have good years and bad years. If we plotted performance by age for any one player, we would not expect the points to lie on a smooth curve as in the figure. Good years would be above the curve, and bad years would be below it. In general, however, we would expect the points to rise for a while and then decline. We would not, for example, expect the points in general to keep rising until the player retired (assuming the player played many years). Another problem is that players differ in ability. They have different lifetime levels of performance. One curve in Figure 9-1 does not fit all.

To estimate aging effects in baseball, we need to make further assumptions than simply that players get better for a while and then get worse. We need more theory—more theoretical restrictions. We will make two further assumptions. The first is that the shape of the curve is quadratic going up and quadratic going down but not necessarily the same quadratic. The curve in Figure 9-1 is in fact this shape, where the first quadratic rises faster than the second quadratic falls. The second assumption is that this curve pertains to all players except for the height of the curve. Better players have higher curves but the same shape.

These two assumptions may or may not be good approximations to reality, and we will have more to say about this later. For now, the aim is to estimate the two quadratic curves and the peak age in Figure 9-1 along with the height of the curve for each player.

The Data

Baseball is a discipline that has terrific data. Almost every minute played in a game has been recorded, and data are available back to the beginning of the sport. We will use a subset of these data. Yearly data on every player who played major league baseball from 1871 on are available from http://baseball.com. We use games played from 1921 through 2004. The year 1921 is the first year of the "live" ball. Only players who have played at least 10 "full-time" years in this period are included in the sample, where a full-time year is defined as one in which a batter played in at least 100 games and a pitcher pitched at least 450 outs. (Almost all relief pitchers are excluded from the sample because almost no relief pitcher pitches as many as 450 outs a year.) The aim of this chapter is to estimate aging effects for injury-free, career baseball players, and the sample was chosen with this in mind. If a batter played fewer than 100 games or a (nonrelief) pitcher pitched fewer than 450 outs in a year, it is possible that the player was injured, and so these "part-time" years were excluded. If a player played at least 10 full-time years, he is clearly a career player. The estimated aging effects in this chapter are thus conditional on the player being a career player and not affected by injuries. No attempt is made to estimate the effect of aging on injuries. The sample for batters includes 441 players and 5,596 observations (total number of years played by all 441 players). The sample for pitchers includes 144 players and 1,809 observations.

Players who are included in the sample may have played nonfulltime years, but these years for the player are not in the sample. Players who played beyond 2004 are included in the sample if they have 10 fulltime years from 2004 back. Players who began playing prior to 1921 are included if they have 10 full-time years from 1921 forward, but their observations prior to 1921 are not included even if the observations are for full-time years because no observations before 1921 are used.

Having chosen the players, we now need to choose the measure of performance. Consider batters first. A common measure of performance for a batter is his batting average, namely, hits divided by at bats. Many baseball experts, however, consider on-base percentage (OBP) a better measure of a player's performance—of his contribution to the team— and we will use this measure. OBP is equal to (hits plus bases on balls plus hit by pitch) divided by (at bats plus bases on balls plus hit by pitch plus sacrifice flies). OBP is the percentage of time when a player comes up to bat that he either gets a hit, walks, or is hit by a pitch.

Another measure of performance that baseball experts like is called OPS. OPS is equal to OBP plus slugging percentage, where slugging percentage is (hits plus doubles plus 2 times triples plus 3 times home runs) divided by at bats. OPS gives more weight to extra base hits than does OBP. It weights power hitting more. We will also present estimates using OPS.

For pitchers, the most popular measure of performance is earned run average (ERA), and we will use this measure. ERA is equal to the number of earned runs allowed divided by (the number of outs made divided by 27).

The only other variable needed is the player's age for each year that he played full time. Data are available on each player's birth date, and a player's age for a given year was taken to be the year in question minus the player's birth year. Age is thus taken to be an integer.

Fit the Data

As depicted in Figure 9-1, if the two quadratics at the peak age both have zero slopes and touch each other, there are three coefficients to estimate. One is the peak age, one is the shape of the left quadratic, and one is the shape of the right quadratic. In addition, as discussed earlier, each player has his own height of the curve. For batters, there are 441 players, so there are 441 heights to estimate. There is in effect a coefficient assigned to each player, namely, the height. For pitchers, there are 144 height coefficients to estimate.

The fitting procedure for batters using the OPS measure of performance is as follows. For a given shape of the curve, which is determined by the three coefficients, and for a given height for each player, the predicted OPS for each player at each age that he played can be computed. The predicted value is just the point on the curve at the given age and the given height for the player. As noted above, there are 5,596 total observations (441 players and 10 or more years per player). For each of these observations, we can compute the difference between the actual OPS that the player achieved and the predicted OPS from the curve. This gives us 5,596 errors, which we can square and then add up to get the sum of squared errors. This is the sum of squared errors for the particular curve. We can do this again for a different curve and get a second sum of squared errors and so on.

The fitting problem is to find the curve that gives the smallest sum of squared errors. There are a total of 444 coefficients to estimate: the peak age, the two quadratic coefficients, and the 441 heights. You can think about a computer trying thousands of sets of 444 coefficients, for each set computing the sum of squared errors, and choosing the set that gives the smallest sum. In practice, there are faster ways of doing this, but the answer is the same. We can easily find the best fitting set of coefficients.

It is important to note that this procedure is different from the procedure in the last chapter determining the marathon aging curve. For the marathon work, the aim was to find the biological minimum time at each age for male runners. The record time for each age was used as the observation for that age. For the most part, this was a different person at each age. No actual time at any age should be lower than the predicted time from the curve because the curve is meant to represent the best that any one can do.

In this chapter, we are dealing with particular individuals—441 batters and 144 pitchers. The curve is meant to represent the average performance for each player at each age. If a player has a better than average year regarding, say, OPS, his actual OPS will be above the curve, and conversely if he has a worse than average year. If the fit is good, the actual points will be close to the curve at each age, but some will be above and some will be below. The curve does not represent the biological best that anyone could do at that age. On the other hand, the quadratic improvement rate, the peak age, and the quadratic decline rate are meant to be biological estimates. These are estimates of how much players on average improve and decline with age.

The Results

How best to report the results? Of obvious interest is the peak age, one of the three coefficients that determines the curve, and this will be reported. The two quadratic coefficients, on the other hand, are not in themselves very informative. It is hard to go from these coefficients to seeing how flat or steep the curve is. A more informative way of looking at the curve is to take the predicted value from the curve at a given age divided by the predicted value at the peak age. This ratio, which will be called the *performance ratio*, is always less than one since by definition the predicted value at the peak age is the maximum. We will present these ratios for ages 19, 22, 25, 28, 31, 34, 37, 40, and 43. The peak age estimate and these ratios are presented in Table 9-1 for three cases: OPS and OBP for batters and ERA for pitchers.

The table shows that the peak age for batters is about 28 (27.6 for OPS and 28.3 for OBP). For pitchers, the peak age is slightly younger at 26.5. The rate of improvement is faster going up than is the rate of

TABLE **9-1**   Results of estimating the curve in Figure 9-1

Peak Age	PERFORMANCE RATIO: PERCENT OF PEAK								
	19	22	25	28	31	34	37	40	43
	OPS								
27.6	0.899	0.957	0.991	1.000	0.995	0.982	0.962	0.934	0.898
	OBP								
28.3	0.903	0.956	0.988	1.000	0.998	0.990	0.976	0.957	0.932
	ERA								
26.5	0.799	0.917	0.990	0.996	0.963	0.902	0.825	0.739	0.655

NOTES: Average OPS is 0.793; average OBP is 0.354; average ERA is 3.50; standard error is 0.0757 for OPS, 0.0276 for OBP, and 0.6845 for ERA; for OPS and OBP 5,596 observations, 441 players; for ERA 1,809 observations, 144 players.

decline going down. In other words, the left quadratic is steeper than the right. For example, for OPS, the increase from age 19 to the peak age 28 (9 years) is 0.101, whereas the decrease from age 28 to age 37 (9 years) is only 0.038. For OPS, the performance ratio ranges from 0.899 for age 19 to 1.000 for age 28 to 0.898 for age 43. The rate of decline is slightly smaller for OBP, where the performance ratio at age 43 is 0.932. The smaller decline for OBP is consistent with casual observations, which suggests that hitting for power is one of the first things to go.

For pitchers versus batters, the quadratic is steeper going up and steeper going down; age is estimated to have a larger effect on pitchers than on batters in both directions. The performance ratio for pitchers is 0.655 for age 43, a large drop from the peak. Even for age 34, the performance ratio is down to 0.902. For age 22, the performance ratio is also fairly low, at 0.917.

It may be helpful in understanding the results to focus on some individual players. Figure 9-2 plots the results for Ted Williams. The height of the curve is determined by Williams's coefficient—one of the 441 height estimates. You can see that Williams's observations lie around the curve, some above and some below. One of his best years, judged by the distance the actual observation is above the line, was at age 23. One of his worst was at age 41. At age 42, his last year, he was close to the line.

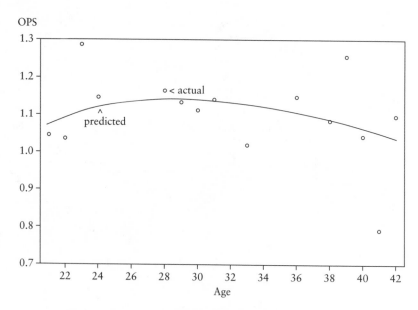

FIGURE **9-2**   Predicted and actual OPS for Ted Williams

What Figure 9-2 shows for Williams, and what the other figures we are about to discuss also show, is that the deviations from the line are large. The range of best OPS to worst OPS is much larger than the range of the predicted line from the largest value (at the peak age) to the smallest value (at the beginning or end of the line). Much of the variation in a player's performance from year to year has nothing to do with his age. This variation shows the need for a large sample to try to estimate aging effects.

You might have thought we could take a player's 15 or so observations and just use them to estimate the four coefficients for that player. For batters, we would then have 441 estimates of the peak age, one per batter, and 441 estimates of each of the other three coefficients. These estimates would, however, vary enormously across players because each estimate would be based on a small number of observations that have a large variation, as Figure 9-2 shows. To get estimates that are at all trustworthy, we need to pool the players, in our case by assuming that the aging curve is the same for all players except for the height. This assumption may, of course, not be a good one, and this is a potential pitfall

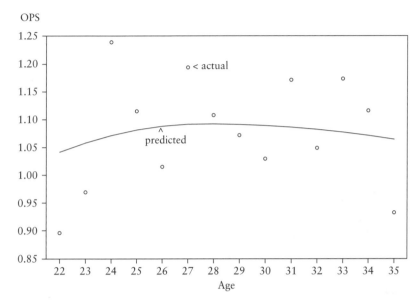

FIGURE **9-3**   Predicted and actual OPS for Lou Gehrig

to be concerned about. But without some assumption like this, it would not be possible to get any useful estimates. We discuss this more in the pitfalls section below.

Figure 9-3 plots the results for Lou Gehrig. One of Gehrig's best years was at age 24, and one of his worst was his last year at age 35. His age 34 performance was close to the line. The height of the predicted line for Williams is slightly larger than the height of the predicted line for Gehrig, so Williams is estimated to be slightly better than Gehrig.

We have just ranked Williams and Gehrig on the basis of their height coefficient, but we can in fact rank all 441 batters and 144 pitchers because each has his own height coefficient. This is done in Table 9-2 for batters and OPS, in Table 9-3 for batters and OBP, and in Table 9-4 for pitchers and ERA. The top 20 players are presented in each case. "Height" in the tables is the estimate of the height coefficient for that player. Each batter has a lifetime OPS and OBP, and each pitcher has a lifetime ERA. We can thus also rank players on the basis of their lifetime numbers, and these rankings are presented in the tables. For example, Rogers Hornsby for OPS ranks 3 regarding his height coefficient but only

TABLE **9-2**   Top twenty batters using OPS

| Batter | FULL TIME & AGE CORRECTED | | LIFETIME | |
	Rank	Height	Rank	OPS
Babe Ruth	1	1.209	1	1.164
Ted Williams	2	1.143	2	1.115
Rogers Hornsby	3	1.105	6	1.010
Lou Gehrig	4	1.093	3	1.080
Barry Bonds	5	1.086	4	1.053
Jimmie Foxx	6	1.055	5	1.038
Manny Ramirez	7	1.036	7	1.010
Harry Heilmann	8	1.025	25	0.930
Frank Thomas	9	1.015	8	0.996
Jim Thome	10	1.013	10	0.979
Mark McGwire	11	1.002	9	0.982
Mickey Mantle	12	1.000	11	0.977
Stan Musial	13	0.999	13	0.976
Joe DiMaggio	14	0.993	12	0.977
Larry Walker	15	0.989	14	0.969
Mel Ott	16	0.985	17	0.947
Edgar Martinez	17	0.982	24	0.933
Johnny Mize	18	0.977	15	0.959
Willie Mays	19	0.974	20	0.941
Ken Griffey Jr.	20	0.971	22	0.937

6 on lifetime OPS. The largest difference is for Harry Heilmann, who ranks 8 using his height coefficient and 25 using his lifetime OPS.

Why the differences in the rankings using the height coefficient versus using the lifetime value? The main reason is that the present rankings are age adjusted. Take two players. Say that one played 10 full-time years and retired at age 33 and the other played 15 full-time years and retired at age 38. The second player played more of his years after the peak age than did the first, and so, other things being equal, the second will have a lower lifetime OPS than the first. The present rankings adjust for this difference. Players are ranked on the height of the curve in Figure 9-1, and it does not matter how many of a player's observations occur before or after the peak age.

Another reason the present rankings may differ from rankings using lifetime measures is that we are only using full-time observations. If

TABLE **9-3**   Top twenty batters using OBP

| Batter | FULL TIME & AGE CORRECTED | | LIFETIME | |
	Rank	Height	Rank	ERA
Ted Williams	1	0.491	1	0.482
Babe Ruth	2	0.488	2	0.474
Rogers Hornsby	3	0.461	5	0.434
Lou Gehrig	4	0.452	3	0.447
Barry Bonds	5	0.449	4	0.443
Harry Heilmann	6	0.441	16	0.409
Jimmie Foxx	7	0.435	7	0.428
Frank Thomas	8	0.434	6	0.429
Edgar Martinez	9	0.431	10	0.418
Mickey Mantle	10	0.429	8	0.420
Mel Ott	11	0.428	13	0.414
Stan Musial	12	0.422	11	0.417
Mickey Cochrane	13	0.422	9	0.419
Jim Thome	14	0.421	15	0.410
Manny Ramirez	15	0.421	14	0.411
Wade Boggs	16	0.418	12	0.415
Elmer Valo	17	0.416	30	0.398
Arky Vaughan	18	0.415	19	0.406
Rickey Henderson	19	0.415	23	0.401
Gary Sheffield	20	0.413	26	0.400

a player played some years but not full time (not 100 games for batters and 450 outs for pitchers), these years count in his lifetime totals but not in the height estimates. These years could be better or worse than average depending on why he played only part time—very young, very old, injured.

Babe Ruth is 1 on OPS and 2 on OBP, and Ted Williams is the opposite. Manny Ramirez is 7 on OPS and only 15 on OBP. Mark McGwire is 11 on OPS and does not make the top 20 on OBP (he is 41). Similarly, Joe DiMaggio is 14 on OPS and does not make the top 20 on OBP (he is 30), and Willie Mays is 19 on OPS and does not make the top 20 on OBP (he is 56). Stan Musial is very even—13 on OPS and 12 on OBP.

The most interesting case is probably Harry Heilmann. He ranks 8 on OPS and 6 on OBP, but lifetime, he only ranks 25 on OPS and 16 on OBP. Why the large differences? Heilmann played 14 full-time years, but 4 of them were before 1921, which are not used for the present rankings but are in the lifetime numbers. It turns out that Heilmann did noticeably better beginning in 1921, which could be due to the introduction of the live ball in 1921. So correcting for age and for the live-ball introduction, Heilmann is one of the best baseball players ever. According to Ira Smith in *Baseball's Famous Outfielders*, Heilmann possessed "many virtues, including loyalty, kindness, tolerance and generosity."

Regarding the pitchers in Table 9-4, Whitey Ford is first in both the present ranking and lifetime ERA. Juan Marichal is 11 in the present ranking but 4 in lifetime ERA. Marichal retired relatively early, and so a higher than average percentage of his years were near the peak age. Age corrected, he thus does not do as well as his lifetime ERA ranking. Phil Niekro is perhaps the most interesting case in the table. He is ranked 10 in the present ranking but only 48 using lifetime ERA. Niekro pitched 24 years, ages 25–48, with all but ages 25, 26, 27, 42, and 48 being full time. Niekro is way above average regarding the number of years played

TABLE **9-4**   Top twenty pitchers using ERA

| Pitcher | FULL TIME & AGE CORRECTED | | LIFETIME | |
	Rank	Height	Rank	ERA
Whitey Ford	1	2.669	1	2.745
Tom Seaver	2	2.671	3	2.862
Bob Gibson	3	2.673	5	2.915
Jim Palmer	4	2.718	2	2.856
Mike Cuellar	5	2.792	14	3.138
Lefty Grove	6	2.812	10	3.058
Warren Spahn	7	2.850	12	3.086
Gaylord Perry	8	2.851	13	3.105
Greg Maddux	9	2.863	7	2.949
Phil Niekro	10	2.864	48	3.351
Juan Marichal	11	2.874	4	2.889
Carl Hubbell	12	2.883	8	2.978
Randy Johnson	13	2.904	11	3.068
Don Drysdale	14	2.909	6	2.948
Nolan Ryan	15	2.939	20	3.193
Dazzy Vance	16	2.954	27	3.240
Roger Clemens	17	2.963	18	3.181
Hal Newhouser	18	2.975	9	3.055
Dutch Leonard	19	3.006	29	3.250
Dave McNally	20	3.025	26	3.237

after the peak age, and so age correcting his performance makes a big difference. (For those of you who are wondering, Sandy Koufax is not on the list because he played only 9 full-time years.)

Possible Pitfalls

As discussed in Chapter 2, a common procedure in statistical work is to examine the sensitivity of results to various assumptions that have been made. How robust are the conclusions to changes in the assumptions? The following are some examples of this procedure.

Consider batters first. We have defined full time as playing 100 games per year, and we have included players who played 10 full-time years. For one check, we changed the definition of full time to be 80 games per year and included players who played 8 full-time years according to this definition. This gave 932 players rather than 441 and 10,605 observations rather than 5,596. The sample is thus considerably larger. We then redid the results using this larger sample. Although not presented here, this change had a very small effect on the results for either OPS or OBP. None of the conclusions were altered in any important ways.

Another change was to drop all observations in which a player was older than 37 years (but keeping a player in, even if this resulted in fewer than 10 full-time years for the player). This resulted in the same number of players (441) but 5,380 observations rather than 5,596. This likewise had very little effect on the results.

For pitchers, we included anyone in the sample who played 8 full-time years (rather than 10) but kept the definition of a full-time year as 450 outs. This yielded 260 players rather than 144 and 2,775 observations rather than 1,809. This change led to the estimate of the peak age falling from 26.5 to 24.0, and so the estimates are somewhat sensitive to the addition of more pitchers. The shapes of the quadratics were, however, only slightly changed.

For another change, all observations in which a pitcher was older than 37 years were dropped. This results in the same number of pitchers (144) but 1,615 observations rather than 1,809. For this change, the estimate of the peak age was 25.2 rather than 26.5, so again the estimates are somewhat sensitive to the age cutoff. The shapes of the quadratics were only slightly changed.

These checks thus show that overall the results are not very sensitive to adding more players and deleting older ages. The results for pitchers are more sensitive than the results for batters, but none of the basic conclusions changed, even for pitchers.

Another possible pitfall is that no adjustments have been made to the introduction of the designated hitter rule in the American League in 1973, the different ballparks that players play in, and different league yearly averages. It may be that a player's performance in a given year is affected by whether or not there is a designated hitter rule, which ballparks he plays in, and how in general players are doing that year. It is difficult to adjust for these differences, and no attempt was made to do this here. Note, however, that we do not require that the entire period between 1921 and 2004 be stable. Each player plays roughly 15 years, and we require that the 15-year period in which he plays be stable. This is clearly a better assumption for a player who plays most of his years with one team than for a player who moves around a lot, particularly between leagues. In general, the assumption may not be a bad approximation, but no attempt is made to test it here.

Another possible pitfall is that players may not all be the same regarding the peak age and the shape of the curve in Figure 9-1. There may be, for example, *ageless wonders*, who slow down very little as they age. We could estimate a completely different curve for each player (for batters, 441 different curves). The problem with this, as discussed earlier, is that there would be very few observations per estimated curve—generally less than 15. Very little confidence could be placed on the estimates of any one curve. By assuming that all players are the same except for the height of the curve, we gain the ability to estimate the peak age and the quadratic coefficients fairly precisely (many observations per estimated coefficient) but again at a cost that the assumption may not be a good approximation.

Figures 9-2 and 9-3 show that Williams and Gehrig are not ageless wonders. For them, there is no systematic pattern of the actual observations lying considerably above the line at the older ages. We can search for ageless wonders by simply looking for players who have many observations above the line at the older ages. If we find many of these players, this would suggest that the assumption of no ageless wonders may not be a good approximation.

We searched for ageless wonders in the following way using the OPS curve. For a given player and year, the difference between his actual OPS and the OPS predicted by the estimated curve was recorded. Call this difference an *error*. Positive errors mean that the player did better than predicted, and negative errors mean the opposite. We then looked at all the large positive errors after the estimated peak age of 27.6. "Large" is defined as an error greater than the standard error. (Remember that the standard error is a measure of the average error across all observations.) A player was then chosen (as an ageless wonder) if he had four or more of these large positive errors after the peak age. There were only 17 such players out of 441, which is encouraging for the assumption of no ageless wonders. Only a few players are large outliers. You might ask who are these 17 players, and this is the subject of the next section.

Ageless Wonders or Steroids?

Of the 17 players found with large positive errors at older ages, there were only 3 who did not play more than half of their careers in the 1990s and beyond. The period searched was 1921–2004, and so this concentration is unusual. The three players who played earlier than the 1990s are Bob Boone, Dwight Evans, and Charlie Gehringer. The other 14 in alphabetical order are Albert Belle, Barry Bonds, Ken Caminiti, Chili Davis, Steve Finley, Julio Franco, Gary Gaetti, Andres Galarraga, Luis Gonzalez, Mark McGwire, Paul Molitor, Sammy Sosa, B. J. Surhoff, and Larry Walker.

By far, the most impressive player regarding end-of-career performance is Barry Bonds. Figure 9-4 plots the observations for Bonds. You can see that his last four errors (distances from his actual OPS to his predicted OPS on the line), which correspond to ages 37–40, are very large. Three of these errors are the largest in the sample period of 5,596 observations, and the last one is 5.5 times the standard error.

Figure 9-5 plots the observations for Mark McGwire. You can see that four of his last five errors are large. Three of these are larger than two standard errors (age 33 in 1996, age 35 in 1998, and age 36 in 1999). Not counting Bonds, Sammy Sosa has the largest error (age 33 in 2001), and Luis Gonzales has the second largest (age 34 in 2001). (Figures are not

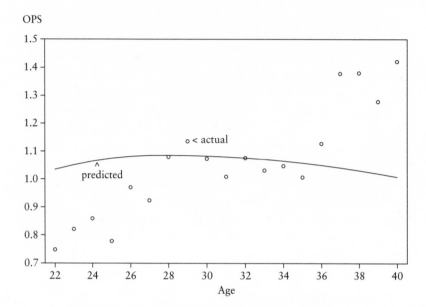

FIGURE **9-4**   Predicted and actual OPS for Barry Bonds

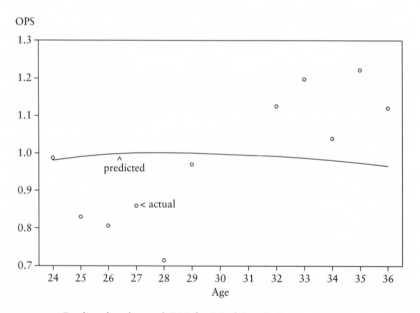

FIGURE **9-5**   Predicted and actual OPS for Mark McGwire

presented for these two. The error patterns are similar as those for Bonds and McGwire but not as extreme.)

An obvious question is whether error patterns like those for Bonds and McGwire are due to the use of steroids or other performance-enhancing drugs. We have to be careful here. Patterns like these are not smoking guns: we have no direct evidence from the present analysis on drug use. Also, we would expect that just by chance some players would have this pattern of errors. For example, it seems unlikely from what we know that Charlie Gehringer, who played between 1926 and 1941, used performance-enhancing drugs. Figure 9-6 plots the observations for Gehringer. You can see that his errors at the older ages are all positive except for the last one and that some of them are large. This looks suspicious, but in this case, it is unlikely to be due to drug use. Regarding Andres Galarraga, who did play in the 1990s, four of his six large errors occurred when he was playing for Colorado, 1993–1997, which has a hitter-friendly ballpark. This could be the reason he made the search list. Also, all four of Larry Walker's large errors occurred when he was playing for Colorado, which was between 1995 and 2003.

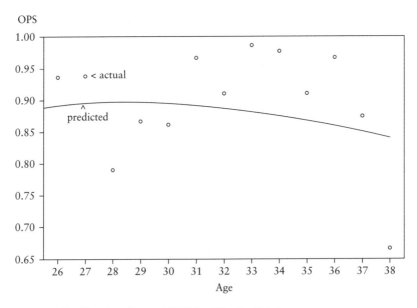

FIGURE **9-6**   Predicted and actual OPS for Charlie Gehringer

Regarding possible drug use, you can look at plots with a pattern like that in Figures 9-4 and 9-5 for Bonds and McGwire as background detective work. Patterns like this are suspicious and call for further investigation. But there needs to be other evidence before any accusations should be made. Note also that the fact that some player does not show up in the search list does not mean he never took performance-enhancing drugs. Players may take such drugs, but the drugs don't do much good.

Are Older Players Overpaid?

The estimated peak-performance ages in Table 9-1 are fairly young—27.9 for OPS, 28.3 for OBP, and 26.5 for ERA. Also, the estimated rates of decline after the peak age are not trivial at the older ages. Do baseball owners and general managers take this into account when deciding players' contracts and when deciding which new players to hire? In particular, do baseball owners underestimate rates of decline when deciding salaries and lengths of contracts? This question is beyond the scope of this chapter, but a table like Table 9-1 could be useful for contract negotiations. What could be done would be to update the estimates through the latest year and use the estimated curve and the estimated height of the curve for a given player to predict how the player should perform in the following year. (The player would need to have played 10 full-time years to be in the sample unless the 10-year cutoff was made smaller.) This would be the player's predicted performance under the assumption that he has an average year. In practice, of course, he will do either better or worse than this. But this prediction could be used as a guide to the negotiations.

Finally, it should be noted that some aging players may be paid more than their predicted performance would warrant, even if the predicted performance were known. Popular players who have played for a team for a long time may have considerable fan loyalty—think Derek Jeter and the Yankees—which helps attendance and thus helps revenue. Owners will obviously take this into account in deciding how much a player is worth to them.

Conclusion

We have used the tools from Chapter 2 to analyze aging effects in baseball. The curve in Figure 9-1 has been estimated for 441 batters and

144 pitchers. Once the estimates have been obtained, they can be used to rank the players and to check for unusual patterns at the older ages. The ranking has the advantage of correcting for age differences across careers. It is also possible that the estimates could be helpful in contract negotiations. Tables 9-2, 9-3, and 9-4 list only the top 20 players. For baseball aficionados, all 441 batters and 144 pitchers are ranked in the paper listed in the Chapter Notes. We now move on to college football.

Luck is not chance–
It's Toil–
Fortune's expensive smile
Is earned–
The Father of the Mine
Is that old-fashioned Coin
We spurned–

> *Emily Dickinson,* Luck is not chance

Background and Theory

Each week during the college football season, there are many rankings of the Division I-A teams. Some rankings are based on votes of sportswriters, and some are based on computer algorithms. The computer algorithms take into account things like won–loss record, margin of victory, strength of schedule, and strength of individual conferences. Since 1998, a subset of the computer rankings has been used in tandem with the Associated Press and ESPN/USA Today writers' polls by the NCAA and the Bowl Championship Series (BCS) to determine which two teams play in the national championship game.

Each ranking system uses a different algorithm, and since the introduction of the BCS by the NCAA, there has been much controversy concerning which is the best system for determining which teams play in the national championship game. For example, in 2002, the NCAA decided that any system that included margin of victory in its algorithm would be dropped for the upcoming 2002–2003 season. The algorithms are generally fairly complicated, and there is no easy way to summarize their main differences. Each system more or less starts with a team's won–loss record and makes adjustments from there.

Available each week aside from the rankings are betting spreads for each upcoming game. Las Vegas, for example, has a very active betting market for college football games. Say, for example, that Oklahoma is playing Texas, and the betting spread is 6.5 points in favor of Oklahoma. If you bet on Oklahoma, you win if Oklahoma wins by 7 points or more. If you bet on Texas, you win if Texas wins outright or loses by 6 points or fewer.

An interesting question is how good the ranking systems and the betting markets are at predicting games. Possibly, for example, all the systems and markets contain the same useful information, and on average all do the same. Or maybe some particular system contains more useful information than all the other systems and more than the betting markets, in which case it will on average do the best. Or perhaps the betting markets contain more useful information, in which case the betting markets will do the best.

We can in fact examine, using the tools in this book, a more complicated question than simply which market or system does best. Possibly, one system has useful information for predicting games that another system does not have, but the other system has useful information that the first system does not have. We can test for this. Furthermore, if both systems have independent useful information, there are combinations of the predictions from the two systems that are better than each system individually, and we can find the best combination.

To give away the punch line, we obtain two exciting results. The first is that we find useful independent information in five computer ranking systems. The best combination of the predictions from these five systems does better than any one system by itself. What is exciting about this is that you might think money could be made by using the best combination to bet on games. The best combination might have useful information that the betting markets do not have. For example, if the use of the best combination predicted team A to beat team B by 10 points and if the betting markets had team A winning by 15 points, you should bet on team B. The combination says that team A is not as good as the markets think. If on average the combination is better than the betting markets (contains more useful information), this will be a moneymaking strategy (assuming that the house take does not wipe out the profits).

The second exciting result is that the best combination is not as good as the betting markets. The best combination contains no useful information that the betting markets do not also have, and the betting markets contain useful information that the best combination does not have. There is no money to be made using the best combination even if there were no house take. In this sense, the betting markets are efficient. The betting markets incorporate all useful information that is known at the time of the game. So the tools used in this chapter reveal some exciting results, but they will not make you any money.

We are thus examining two questions. The first is whether the computer ranking systems contain useful independent information, and the second is whether the best combination contains useful information that the betting markets do not have. The answer to the first is yes, and the answer to the second is no.

The Data

Data on six ranking systems were collected. The six systems are (1) Matthews/Scripps Howard (MAT), (2) Jeff Sagarin's *USA Today* (SAG), (3) Richard Billingsley (BIL), (4) *Atlanta Journal-Constitution* Colley Matrix (COL), (5) Kenneth Massey (MAS), and (6) Dunkel (DUN). In addition, there is a seventh system that uses *only* won–loss records. This system will be denoted REC.

Data were collected for four years, 1998, 1999, 2000, and 2001, and for 10 weeks per year beginning with week 6. (1998 is the first year of the BCS.) This resulted in a total of 1,582 games. For 2001, there were 117 Division I-A teams; for 2000, there were 115 teams; for 1999, there were 114 teams; and for 1998, there were 112 teams.

The data were obtained from various Web sites. Most of the rankings were obtained from Kenneth Massey's site: http://www.masseyratings .com/cf/compare.htm. The rankings for COL were obtained from http:// www.colleyrankings.com. The scores of the games for the 1998 and 1999 seasons were obtained from http://www.cae.wisc.edu/~dwilson/rsfc /history/howell, and the scores of the games for the 2000 and 2001 seasons were obtained from http://cbs.sportsline.com. Data from these last two sites were also collected on which team (if either) was the home team.

The variable to be explained is the actual point spread in a game, which will be denoted SPREAD. For each game, we assign one team to be the first team, denoted team A, with the other team denoted team B. If team A beat team B 28 to 13, the point spread is 15. If team B beat team A 28 to 13, the point spread is –15. As noted above, there are a total of 1,582 games in the sample, so there are 1,582 observations on SPREAD. We also constructed a home field variable, denoted H, which is taken to be 1 if team A is the home team, –1 if team B is the home team, and 0 if neither team is the home team (as for bowl games).

Regarding the rankings systems, they do not predict games; they simply rank teams. We use a system's rankings for the week to create what we will call a *prediction variable* for each game for the week for that system. This variable is simply the difference in the rankings. If, for example, Stanford is ranked 10 and UCLA is ranked 21 and if Stanford plays UCLA that week, the prediction variable for this game has a value of 11 if Stanford is team A and –11 if UCLA is team A. The prediction variable will be denoted by the name of the ranking system—MAT, SAG, BIL, COL, MAS, and DUN. For the system that uses only won–loss records (REC), the prediction variable is taken to be (in percentage points) the percentage to date of games won by team A minus the percentage won by team B. For example, if team A has won 80 percent of its games and team B has won 60 percent, the value of the prediction variable is 20.

It is important to note that none of the prediction variables uses information on home field for the games. It is thus not necessarily the case that a positive value for the prediction variable implies that the people running the system would predict team A to beat team B if they were forced to make a prediction. If team A were ranked only slightly ahead of team B and if team B had home field advantage, team B might be predicted to win. As discussed below, we adjust for this by adding the home field variable, H.

The Results

Table 10-1 presents the results. In the first row, SPREAD is taken to depend only on H, the home field variable, and MAT, the prediction variable from computer ranking system MAT. The fitting exercise is to find the coefficient for MAT and the coefficient for H that leads to the best fit—the smallest sum of squared errors. There are 1,582 observations. The question being asked is whether MAT is significant in explaining SPREAD after taking into account the home field variable. The answer is yes. The *t*-statistic for MAT is 27.72, and so MAT is significant. The home field variable is also significant with a *t*-statistic of 10.26. The coefficient for H is 4.52, which means that the home field advantage is 4.52 points. The standard error is 16.95 points. Another measure of fit in this context is the percentage of the 1,582 games that were predicted correctly as to the winner. For the first row, 70.7 percent of the games were predicted correctly regarding winner.

Rows 2 through 7 look at each of the other ranking systems individually. Each is significant. Even REC, which uses only won–loss information, is significant with a *t*-statistic of 23.90, a standard error of 17.71 points, and 69.1 percent of the games predicted correctly. The best system in terms of fit is SAG, with a standard error of 16.71 points and 71.9 percent of the games predicted correctly. The coefficient for H does not vary much down the seven rows. It ranges from 4.13 to 4.70, and so it looks like that the home field advantage is around 4.5 points. The average total point score (team A's points plus team B's points) across all 1,582 games is 52 points per game, and so in percentage terms, the home field advantage is between about 8 and 9 percent of the total points.

Each ranking system thus looks good by itself. Each is significant. We can now ask our first exciting question: is there useful *independent* information in the different systems? We answer this question by simply including in the explanation of SPREAD all seven of the ranking systems' prediction variables plus H. The results are in row 8. If a prediction variable is significant in this row, it means that it has useful predictive information that is not in the other prediction variables. Even with all the other prediction variables included, it contributes significantly to the explanation of SPREAD.

In row 8, MAT and MAS are not significant, but the others are. For the results in row 9, we have dropped MAT and MAS and reestimated with these two variables dropped. We will focus on row 9. The home field coefficient has not changed much. It is 4.30 with a *t*-statistic of 9.93. The *t*-statistics of the five prediction variables are 5.38, 2.17, –4.25, 3.53, and 3.89. The last *t*-statistic of 3.89 is for REC, which just uses won–loss information. This means that there is useful information in the won–loss records that is not being used by the other systems.

The coefficient for COL is negative (–.171) with a *t*-statistic of –4.25. COL thus contributes significantly to the explanation of SPREAD

TABLE **10-1** Testing the ranking systems (dependent variable is SPREAD)

	H	MAT	SAG	BIL	COL	MAS	DUN	REC	SE	% right
1	4.52 (10.26)	.314 (27.72)							16.95	.707
2	4.13 (9.50)		.320 (28.94)						16.71	.719
3	4.44 (10.06)			.344 (27.62)					16.97	.710
4	4.62 (10.14)				.273 (24.87)				17.52	.693
5	4.21 (9.63)					.315 (28.49)			16.80	.721
6	4.70 (10.80)						.324 (28.81)		16.73	.707
7	4.69 (10.18)							.313 (23.90)	17.71	.691
8	4.24 (9.75)	-.050 (-0.79)	.217 (3.66)	.073 (2.09)	-.166 (-3.53)	.051 (0.82)	.117 (3.29)	.127 (3.72)	16.46	.729
9	4.30 (9.93)		.217 (5.38)	.075 (2.17)	-.171 (-4.25)		.119 (3.53)	.132 (3.89)	16.46	.729

NOTES: t-statistics are in parentheses; number of observations = 1,582.

but with a negative weight. COL is thus estimated to have independent information, where the information is such that given the values of the other prediction variables, the weight for COL is negative. Regarding MAS, which was dropped in going from row 8 to row 9, it is interesting to note that although it has the third lowest standard error when each system is considered by itself, it is estimated to have no independent information when included with the others. The tool used here, namely, including all prediction variables as explanatory variables and estimating the coefficients, allows this kind of result to be seen. The negative result for MAS does not mean that MAS is necessarily a poor predictor when considered in a one-by-one comparison with the others; it just means that MAS has no value added given the other rankings.

The standard error in row 9 is 16.46 points, and 72.9 percent of the games are predicted correctly as to the winner. The coefficients in row 9 are chosen as those that give the best fit—the best explanation of SPREAD, the smallest sum of squared errors. This row will be called the *best combination* of the ranking systems. This row has the smallest standard error of all the rows.

There is some interesting analysis we can do with row 9, but before discussing this, we should consider possible pitfalls.

Possible Pitfalls

In the last chapter, we examined the sensitivity of the baseball results to changes in various assumptions, and we will do the same in this chapter. First, instead of taking SPREAD to be the actual point spread, we took it to be the actual point spread divided by the total number of points scored in the game. In this case, SPREAD is in percentage terms. Second, instead of taking a prediction variable to be the difference in rankings, we took it to be the difference in rankings divided by the total number of Division I-A teams in the year (either 117, 115, 114, or 112). In this case, the prediction variables are in percentage terms. Third, we took the dependent variable to be a simple won–loss variable that had a value of 0.5 if team A won and a value of –0.5 if team A lost. We redid all the results for each change. The results and conclusions were not sensitive to any of these changes. They are robust to these kinds of unit changes in the variables.

Regarding the third change—taking the dependent variable to be a simple won–loss variable—you might ask whether it is a better variable to be explained than the point spread. The answer is probably no because the point spread contains more information. If, say, one system has team A ranked 10 and team B ranked 40 and another system has team A ranked 12 and team B ranked 20, it seems reasonable to assume that the first system is suggesting a larger margin of victory, even though both are suggesting that team A should win. There is, however, a possible problem with using the point spread, which is that a superior team may ease off to avoid embarrassing the other team. In this case, the point spread would not reveal the true strength of the winning team and the true weakness of the losing team. It turns out, however, as just noted, that the conclusions are not sensitive to which dependent variable is used.

Use the Best Combination

Remember that row 9 in Table 10-1 is the best combination. Once we have this combination, we can rank the teams using it. In other words, once we have the rankings from the other systems and the updated won–loss information for a given week, we can create a new ranking using the coefficients in row 9. We do this as follows. Consider Stanford. We compute a score, which is equal to .217 times the SAG ranking of Stanford, plus .075 times the BIL ranking, minus .171 times the COL ranking, plus .119 times the DUN ranking, and plus .132 times the percentage of wins (in percentage points) that Stanford has for the season so far. We do not use H in the calculations. This gives a score value for Stanford. We do this for all the other teams, for example, 117 teams in 2001, which gives 117 scores. We then rank the scores, lowest to highest, and this gives the new ranking. This new ranking has the property that in a one-to-one matchup on a neutral playing field, no team would be predicted by the best combination to lose to a team ranked below it.

As an example, this ranking was done for the last week of 2001 (before the bowl games) using the individual rankings that were available at the time. This ranking is presented in Table 10-2 for the top 30 teams. Also presented in the table for each team are (1) its won–loss record, (2) its ranking by each of the four systems, and (3) the ranking that the BCS chose. The weights from row 9 in Table 10-1 for the ranking systems are

TABLE **10-2** Ranking using row 9 coefficients: Last week of 2001 (before bowl games)

Weights from Row 9		REC .132	SAG .217	BIL .075	COL −.171	DUN .119	BCS
1	Miami FL	11-0	1	1	1	1	1
2	Nebraska	11-1	3	2	2	5	2
3	Florida	9-2	2	7	8	2	5
4	Texas	10-2	4	10	9	3	7
5	Oklahoma	10-2	6	9	11	6	11
6	Colorado	10-2	5	4	5	4	3
7	Oregon	10-1	7	3	3	10	4
8	Maryland	10-1	11	5	10	15	10
9	Illinois	10-1	12	6	6	18	8
10	Tennessee	10-2	8	8	4	13	6
11	Washington State	9-2	10	12	12	20	12
12	Stanford	9-2	9	11	7	23	9
13	Texas Tech	7-4	19	24	29	9	29
14	Virginia Tech	8-3	24	18	27	11	21
15	LSU	9-3	18	14	13	8	13
16	Kansas State	6-5	14	36	30	7	39
17	Florida State	7-4	16	21	25	16	22
18	Fresno State	11-2	15	29	14	25	19
19	Georgia	8-3	22	17	20	17	18
20	Syracuse	9-3	20	16	16	19	17
21	Michigan	8-3	17	23	18	21	16
22	Southern California	6-5	26	25	37	12	40
23	Ohio State	7-4	30	20	31	14	25
24	UCLA	7-4	13	27	21	28	23
25	South Carolina	8-3	23	19	19	26	14
26	Brigham Young	12-1	21	13	17	54	20
27	Washington	8-3	25	15	15	31	15
28	Oregon State	5-6	41	37	60	24	42
29	Alabama	6-5	32	38	39	22	41
30	North Carolina State	7-4	40	35	41	27	34

also presented. It is interesting to note that because COL has a negative weight, when it ranks a team high, this has, other things being equal, a negative effect on the new ranking and vice versa. For example, Oklahoma is ranked higher than it otherwise would be because COL ranked it fairly low. Overall, SAG has the most influence on the new ranking since it has the largest coefficient.

A ranking like the one just done, which is based on the best combination, is a candidate for the BCS to use in its decision-making process. This ranking uses in an optimal way information in all the ranking systems. The individual ranking systems contain useful independent information, and they can be combined to obtain a better ranking.

Might there be money to be made from this analysis? You could update the best combination each week after obtaining the individual rankings for the week. Given the new data, the coefficients for the best combination could be reestimated, a new ranking could be computed using these coefficients, and from this ranking, a prediction variable could be computed for each upcoming game (adding the home field coefficient when appropriate). You could then bet on a game based on the value of the prediction variable for that game. This would be using more information than any one ranking system has (as well as using the home field information). What could be better than the best combination? We will now see that there is something better.

Betting Markets

Las Vegas has huge betting markets. Data for all 1,582 games on the final Las Vegas line point spread, denoted LV, were obtained from the Gold Sheet Web site, http://goldsheet.com. This would be the betting line that you could use to bet based on the predictions using the best combination. The second exciting question that our tools can answer is whether the best combination or in fact any combination of prediction variables contains useful information not in the Las Vegas line point spread. This can be done by simply adding the LV variable to row 9 in Table 10-1 and computing new estimates. If any variable other than LV is significant, it contains useful independent information.

The results of adding LV to row 9 are presented in Table 10-3. You can see that only LV is significant with a t-statistic of 13.37. Even the

TABLE **10-3**   Adding the betting spread

LV	H	SAG	BIL	COL	DUN	REC	SE	% right
1.030	0.77	.051	−.017	−.065	−.030	.055	15.60	.747
(13.37)	(1.57)	(1.27)	(−0.51)	(−1.67)	(−0.88)	(1.70)		

home field variable is not significant. Although not shown in Table 10-3, when LV was added to each of the other rows in Table 10-1, it was always significant, and none of the other variables were. The results thus show that LV contains all the useful information in the other variables plus more. No computer ranking system or combination of systems has any useful predictive information regarding actual point spreads not in the final Las Vegas point spread. In this sense, the betting markets are efficient.

Each year, the *Yale Daily News* asks Yale faculty their predictions of the Harvard–Yale football game—arguably the most important football game in the United States each year. The aim is to elicit witty responses from the faculty. I am never witty. I just tell the reporter that the best prediction of the game is what the betting markets are saying.

To end on a positive note about the best combination, the fact that it contains no useful information not in the Las Vegas point spread does not mean that it cannot be used to improve the college ranking each week, as discussed above. Not enough information from the betting markets is available to rank the colleges, even the top colleges, and the ranking using the best combination is perhaps the best alternative.

11 Interest Rates

This is a song to celebrate banks,
Because they are full of money and you go into them and all you hear is
  clinks and clanks,
Or maybe a sound like the wind in the trees on the hills,
Which is the rustling of the thousand dollar bills.
Most bankers dwell in marble halls,
Which they get to dwell in because they encourage deposits and discour-
  age withdrawals,
And particularly because they all observe one rule which woe betides the
  banker who fails to heed it,
Which is you must never lend any money to anybody unless they don't
  need it.

> *Ogden Nash, from* Bankers Are Just Like Anybody Else,
> Except Richer

There is a lot of macroeconomics in this chapter and the next, a subject that is not everyone's cup of tea. This chapter discusses interest rates, and the next one discusses inflation. Interest rates are something you should be excited about because they have important effects on people's lives. We will see that the chairman of the Federal Reserve (the Fed) plays an important role in the story in this chapter. The chairman is considered one of the most powerful people in the world. So please read on. Macroeconomics is more exciting than you might think.

There are many kinds of interest rates. If you have a savings account in a bank, you earn interest at the interest rate that the bank pays. If you have a mortgage, you pay interest at the mortgage rate you agreed to when you took out the mortgage. If you buy a corporate bond, you earn interest at the corporate bond rate. Some interest rates are for a short period of time, such as three months or a year. Other interest rates are longer term. A mortgage rate may be for 20 to 30 years, and a corporate bond rate may be for 10 to 15 years.

The interest rate that we are concerned with in this chapter is for a period of three months, and it is called the three-month Treasury bill rate. Part of the debt of the U.S. government is in the form of three-month securities, and it is the interest rate on these securities that we will explain. For shorthand, we will call the three-month Treasury bill rate just the *bill rate*.

Now things get more interesting. How is the bill rate determined? For all intents and purposes, it is determined by the chairman of the Fed. About every six weeks the Federal Open Market Committee (FOMC) of the Federal Reserve meets to set the value of the interest rate. The interest rate that the Fed actually controls is called the *federal funds rate*, which is an overnight interest rate at which commercial banks borrow and lend to each other. The Fed controls this rate by buying and selling government securities in the private market. The chairman of the Fed has enormous influence in the FOMC meetings, and it is extremely rare for the FOMC to do something that the chairman does not want to do.

When the Fed changes the federal funds rate, other interest rates change as well. There is almost a one-for-one change in the three-month Treasury bill rate, and because of this, we will assume in this chapter that the Fed also controls the bill rate. Although not necessarily one for one, changes in the federal funds rate also lead to changes in interest rates like those on savings accounts, corporate bonds, and mortgages. Interest rates in other countries also generally change when U.S. interest rates change. The decision that the Fed makes every six weeks about the federal funds rate thus has an effect on many interest rates.

Why are interest rates a big deal? This chapter is not a primer on macroeconomics, but a few things should be said about the effects of interest rates on the economy. First, interest rates have an effect on stock prices. If you follow the stock market, you know that market analysts hang on every word the Fed chairman says, looking for clues as to whether he will raise or lower interest rates in the future. Generally, high interest rates are bad for stock prices, and low interest rates are good.

Second, interest rates affect the demand for housing. If mortgage rates are high, it is costly to borrow money to buy a new house, and fewer people choose to do so. Fewer new houses are then built. Third, interest rates also affect the demand for large items like cars and refrigerators. If interest rates are high, it is again costly to borrow money to buy these items, and fewer people choose to do so.

Fourth, interest rates affect the plant and equipment investment of firms. If interest rates are high, it is costly for firms to borrow money to finance new investment projects, and fewer investment projects are undertaken.

Finally, interest rates affect consumer spending through their effect on stock prices. Since households own stocks, when stock prices rise, household wealth rises. A fraction of this increase in wealth is spent by households each year, and so a rise in wealth leads to a rise in consumer spending. A fall in interest rates can thus stimulate consumer spending by first stimulating stock prices. Conversely, a rise in interest rates decreases consumer spending by first depressing stock prices.

All this means that an increase in interest rates has a negative effect on expenditures on consumer goods, expenditures on housing, and investment in plant and equipment. Conversely, a decrease in interest rates has a positive effect. Fed policy thus has an important influence on the economy. Since the U.S. economy affects the economies of other countries, Fed policy also has an influence on those economies as well.

I hope this has given you a sense that Fed policy is important in everyone's economic life. The aim of this chapter, however, is not to explain the effects of Fed policy on the economy. Rather, we are interested in what motivates the Fed to do what it does. Just as we have tried to explain the behavior of voters regarding votes for president and the behavior of married individuals regarding how much time (if any) to spend in an affair, we will try to explain the behavior of the Fed. Why does the Fed at times raise interest rates and at times lower them? If we can explain this behavior, we can then use the results to predict what the Fed will do in the future. As usual, we begin with a theory, move to the data, test, think about pitfalls, examine the results, and then predict.

A Theory of Fed Behavior

It is no secret that monetary authorities around the world, including the Fed, hate inflation. One of the main goals of any monetary authority is to keep inflation in check, and for some monetary authorities—although not the Fed—this is the only goal. How does the Fed try to keep inflation in check? We discuss inflation in the next chapter, where we will see that inflation is affected by demand pressure in the economy. Other things being equal, when overall demand in the economy rises, inflation rises, and when overall demand falls, inflation falls. Since the Fed affects overall demand by changing interest rates, it also indirectly affects inflation because demand affects inflation. Therefore, if inflation is higher than the Fed would like, the Fed can raise interest rates to bring inflation down. Inflation is thus likely to have an effect on the Fed's interest setting behavior.

The Fed, however, cares about things other than inflation. In particular, it cares about unemployment. If unemployment is high, many people are looking for a job and cannot find one, which is not a good thing. The Fed can lower unemployment by lowering interest rates, thus stimulating overall demand. If demand increases, the total output produced in the economy increases, and this in turn increases employment because workers are needed to produce the additional output. Thus, the unemployment rate is likely to have an effect on the Fed's interest setting behavior. If the unemployment rate is higher than the Fed would like, it can lower interest rates to bring unemployment down.

If this theory is right, the bill rate (which the Fed for all intents and purposes controls) should depend on inflation and the unemployment rate. Is there anything else? We will see that there are other variables that appear to affect Fed behavior, but the main two are clearly inflation and the unemployment rate. If you remember just these two, you know most of what influences Fed behavior.

The Fed is also concerned about the growth of the money supply. (The *money supply* is roughly the amount of cash in circulation and the amount in checking accounts.) If the money supply has been growing rapidly in the past, the Fed may fear that this will lead to inflation in the future. In other words, the Fed may care about past money supply growth because it cares about future inflation. The past growth of the money supply may thus have a positive effect on the Fed's interest setting behavior. For example, a large past growth of the money supply may lead to Fed to raise interest rates.

There is a period in U.S. history when the Fed, chaired by Paul Volcker, announced that it was mostly concerned about the money supply. Volcker was chairman of the Fed between the third quarter of 1979 and the second quarter of 1987, and the period for which the announcement was relevant is the fourth quarter of 1979 through the third quarter of 1982. This period will be called the *early Volcker period*. We would expect the money supply variable to have more of an effect on the bill rate in this period than either before or after, and we will see that this is the case.

A key characteristic of Fed behavior is a tendency to change interest rates in small steps. If, for example, the Fed is in the process of raising interest rates, it often does this by raising the federal funds rate by 0.25 percentage points each time the FOMC meets (about every six weeks). The Fed does not appear to like large, abrupt changes in interest rates. This means that the value of the federal funds rate at the time of the meeting has an important effect on the new rate that is set. This is, of course, obvious. When the Fed makes a change, if the size of the change is typically small, then the rate at the time of the meeting has a large effect on the value of the new rate. The Fed's interest setting behavior is thus influenced by the value of the existing rate at the time of the meeting.

There are two other timing issues that are relevant for the question of how fast the Fed changes interest rates. First, we will see that the *change* in the unemployment rate appears to affect Fed behavior. If, for example, the unemployment rate is rising, the Fed appears to lower interest rates, other things being equal. That is, although the Fed tends to change interest rates in small steps, it seems to decrease interest rates faster when the unemployment rate is rising and to increase interest rates faster when the unemployment rate is falling.

The other timing issue concerns past changes in interest rates. The change in the bill rate last quarter and the change in the preceding quarter appear to affect the Fed's current choice of the rate. We will not say much about these timing issues. They are not the most important features of Fed behavior, which are the Fed's concerns with inflation and unemployment, but we will see that the timing variables are significant.

The theory is summarized in Box 11-1. *Lagged* means that the variable is the value for the previous quarter, and *lagged twice* means that the variable is for the quarter before that. The variable *money growth lagged–early Volcker* is equal to money growth lagged during the early Volcker period and zero otherwise. Putting in a separate variable for this period is a way of accounting for the different behavior during the early Volcker period.

BOX **11-1**

bill rate depends on:	
	inflation
	unemployment rate
	change in unemployment rate
	money growth lagged
	money growth lagged—early Volcker
	bill rate lagged
	change in bill rate lagged
	change in bill rate lagged twice

The Data

The data that we need to test the theory are easy to come by. The government compiles data on inflation, the unemployment rate, the money supply, and the bill rate. We will use quarterly data, and the period we consider is the first quarter of 1954 through the second quarter of 2010. There are 226 quarters within this period, and so we have 226 observations.

The data on the unemployment rate and inflation are plotted in Figure 11-1. You can see that inflation was high from the mid-1970s through the early 1980s. (We will examine what caused this in the next chapter.) The unemployment rate was also generally high in this period, as well as around 1958, 1961, the early 1990s, and between 2008 and the end of the sample period.

The bill rate is plotted in Figure 11-2. If you compare Figure 11-1 to Figure 11-2, you can see that the bill rate is generally high when inflation is high, which is consistent with the Fed trying to fight inflation by raising interest rates. After inflation came down in the early 1980s, the Fed lowered the bill rate substantially, an action that is consistent with the Fed trying to bring down the unemployment rate by lowering interest rates. Another good example of this is the period beginning in 2008. The unemployment rate rose rapidly in this period, and the Fed brought the bill rate down to near zero.

We also collected data on the money supply, but since the money supply plays a fairly minor role in the story except for the early Volcker period, we will not present a plot of it.

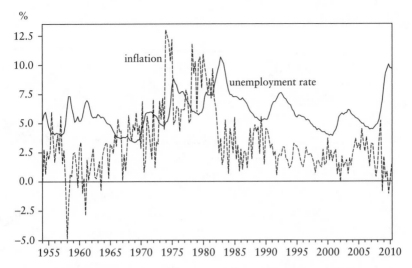

FIGURE **11-1**   The unemployment rate and inflation 1954:1–2010:2

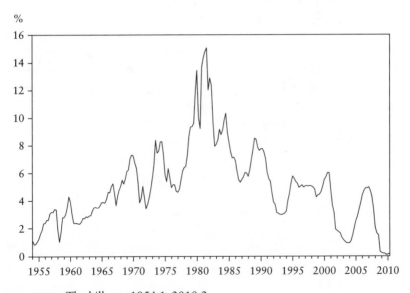

FIGURE **11-2**   The bill rate 1954:1–2010:2

Fit and Test

Given the data, we use a computer to find the set of coefficients that leads to the smallest sum of squared errors. For each set tried, there are 226 errors, so a lot of computation is going on. Before we begin the computations, however, there is one new complication we need to discuss. The theory says that inflation and the unemployment rate affect the bill rate. The Fed changes the bill rate when inflation and the unemployment rate change. However, as we briefly discussed earlier, the bill rate affects inflation and the unemployment rate. For example, when interest rates rise, other things being equal, inflation falls and the unemployment rate rises. We thus have causality in both directions. If we don't do anything about this problem, the best fitting set of coefficients will be biased. Before we use the inflation variable, we need to "purge" the effects of the bill rate on it. Likewise, we need to purge the unemployment rate (and the change in the unemployment rate) from the effects of the bill rate on it. The purged variables can then legitimately be used in explaining the bill rate because their variation is not affected by variations in the bill rate. The following results are based on a method that does this purging. The set of coefficients chosen by the method is based on getting a best fit, and so the insights from Chapter 2 are still relevant. It is just that the best fit in this case is a little different. It is the one that leads to the smallest sum of squared errors using the purged variables as explanatory variables. (As was the case for the method used in Chapter 5, it is beyond the scope of this book to discuss the details of this method.)

The results are shown in Box 11-2. Inflation has a t-statistic of 3.88, the unemployment rate has a t-statistic of −3.39, and the change in the unemployment rate has a t-statistic of −5.71. The three variables are significant. This is thus strong evidence that the Fed looks at inflation and the unemployment rate in setting interest rates.

The coefficient of money growth lagged for other than the early Volcker period is 0.010 with a t-statistic of 2.33. For the early Volcker period, the additional coefficient is 0.223 with a t-statistic of 9.96. The total coefficient for the early Volcker period is thus the sum of these two, or 0.233. This is strong evidence that the Fed put more weight on money growth in the early Volcker period than it has otherwise, a result that is consistent with what the Fed actually said it was doing.

BOX **11-2**

bill rate depends on:		*t*-statistic
0.066	inflation	3.88
−0.082	unemployment rate	−3.39
−0.647	change in unemployment rate	−5.71
0.010	money growth lagged	2.33
0.223	money growth lagged−early Volcker	9.96
0.908	bill rate lagged	58.89
0.279	change in bill rate lagged	5.47
−0.307	change in bill rate lagged twice	−6.43
0.61	intercept	4.44
standard error: 0.47		
number of observations: 226		

The coefficient for the bill rate lagged is 0.908 with a *t*-statistic of 58.89, which is strong evidence that the Fed adjusts slowly. As discussed above, the two changes in bill rate pick up timing effects. They have *t*-statistics of 5.47 and –6.43, respectively, so the two terms are significant.

The standard error is 0.47, which is moderate. It says that 68.2 percent of the time the error in predicting the bill rate should be between –0.47 and 0.47. The highest and lowest values of the bill rate for the 226 observations are 15.09 and 0.06, and 0.47 is quite small relative to this range. On the other hand, the average change (ignoring the sign) in the bill rate from quarter to quarter is 0.47, so the standard error is no smaller than the average quarterly change. (It is just a fluke that the standard error is equal to the average quarterly change.) There are clearly factors that affect Fed behavior other than the variables we have used. We will say more about this later. The main conclusion to be drawn from the results is that inflation and the unemployment rate have highly significant effects on Fed behavior.

Possible Pitfalls

This first part of this section is hard, and it can be skipped if de-sired. An important possible pitfall in the social sciences is that people's behavior can change over time in ways that are not accounted for by the theory. When this happens, we say that behavior is not *stable* over time. There are, fortunately, ways of testing whether behavior is stable, and these ways are the subject matter of the first part of this section. Some of the following discussion is similar to that in Chapter 4 regarding the testing of the weighting restrictions on the economic variables in explaining the House vote shares.

Stability Tests

Probably, the main possible pitfall to worry about in this chapter is whether Fed behavior is different now from what it was in the 1950s, 1960s, and 1970s. We have seen that its behavior was different in the early Volcker period, and it is possible that its behavior after this period was different from its behavior before this period. Remember that the early Volcker period is the fourth quarter of 1979 through the third quarter of 1982. We will use the notation 1979:4 to refer to the fourth quarter of 1979, 1982:3 to refer to third quarter of 1982, and so on. The early Volcker period is thus 1979:4–1982:3.

Let's consider how we can test whether Fed behavior has changed. We will focus on the period before the early Volcker period, which is 1954:1–1979:3, and the period after the early Volcker period, which is 1982:4–2010:2. We will call these two periods the *first* and *second* periods. The middle period (that is, what we've called the *early Volcker period*) is excluded; we know that Fed behavior was different in this period because the Fed said so. If Fed behavior is different between the first and second periods, then at least some of the coefficients are different between the two periods.

How can we test whether the coefficients are different? The main idea is to compare two measures of fit. The first measure is the smallest sum of squared errors that is obtained when we combine the first and second periods. In other words, we find the best fitting set of coefficients using all the observations in the two periods. Call this *measure A*. For the second measure, we treat the two periods separately. We find the best fitting set of coefficients using only observations for the first period and then the best fitting set of coefficients using only observations for the second period. Each of these two sets has associated with it a sum of squared errors for the respective period, and if we add these two sums, we get our second measure of fit, called *measure B*.

Now comes a key point: measure B is always smaller than measure A. We are allowed more flexibility in fitting the data for measure B because we can fit the two periods separately. Measure A forces us to use the same set of coefficients for both periods, but measure B does not. Now, if the true set of coefficients is in fact the same in the two periods (that is, Fed behavior has not changed from the first to the second period), measure B should be only slightly smaller than measure A. On the other hand, if the true set of coefficients is different in the second period than in the first, measure B is likely to be much smaller than measure A. In this case, measure A is incorrectly forced to use a common set of coefficients for both periods, and the fit should not be very good. Therefore, if measure A is much larger than measure B, this suggests that behavior has changed.

We are not finished, however, because we need some way to decide when the difference between measures A and B is large and when it is not. Here we need to go back to thinking about different universes, as we did in Chapters 2 and 4. Assume that Fed behavior has not changed and that the results in Box 11-2 are correct. We know that the size of a typical error is the standard error, which in the box is 0.47. If we assume that the errors come from a bell-shaped curve with standard error of 0.47, we can draw different errors for our second universe. Given these errors, we use the coefficients in Box 11-2 to compute new values of the bill rate. This drawing is similar to the drawing we discussed in Lesson 4 in Chapter 2 in the sense that we are getting a second universe with different errors and then computing different values of the bill rate. Once we have the different bill-rate values, we can compute measure A and measure B and then the difference between the two. These values are different from those obtained using the actual universe because we are using different values of the bill rate. Remember that we are assuming that Fed behavior is unchanged because we are using the coefficients in Box 11-2, which assumes no change in Fed behavior, to calculate the bill-rate values once the errors have been drawn.

Imagine doing this 1,000 times for 1,000 universes. In the end, we have computed 1,000 differences between measures A and B. The next step is to put these differences in order of their size, starting from the largest. We are now almost finished. We take the difference between the two measures that we have computed using the actual data and compare it to the 1,000 differences. Say that this difference is between differences 150 and 151. This says that if the truth is that the weights are valid, we could expect to get a difference as large as ours about 15 percent of the time (150 out of 1,000). This percentage is greater than the usual cutoff of 5 percent, so we would accept the view that the weights are the same. If, on the other hand, the difference in the actual data is between differences 10 and 11, we would reject the view that the weights are valid. In this case, we would expect to get a difference that large only about 1 percent of the time, which is smaller than the 5 percent cutoff.

In practice, stability tests are a little more complicated than this, and the computations can be done without having to draw errors for other universes. The intuition is, however, the same. The view of no change in behavior (stable behavior) is rejected if the difference in fit (that is, the difference between measures like A and B) is large compared to what one would expect to get if the truth were in fact stable behavior.

I used a stability test to see whether there was a change in Fed behavior between the first and second periods, and the case of no change in behavior was not rejected. The computed difference between the two measures (measures like A and B) was such that we could expect to get a value as large as it about 8 percent of the time. The case of no change in Fed behavior is thus not rejected because 8 percent is greater than the cutoff of 5 percent. The results from the test thus support the view that Fed behavior has not changed since 1954 except for the early Volcker period.

Unemployment Rate Versus Output Gap

Another possible pitfall concerns the use of the unemployment rate as an explanatory variable. Another measure of how well the economy is doing is the *output gap*. The output gap is the difference between potential output and actual output. Potential output is an estimate of how much output the economy could produce if there were full employment. The unemployment rate and the output gap are obviously closely related, since unemployment tends to fall as actual output gets closer to potential. In practice, however, the unemployment rate and the output gap are not perfectly related, and the Fed may look at the output gap and not the unemployment rate when setting the interest rate. If this were true, it is likely that the unemployment rate would be significant in explaining the bill rate (which it is) because it would be serving as a proxy for the output gap. We would, of course, be making a mistake since it would actually be the output gap that the Fed is looking at.

We can easily test the output gap versus the unemployment rate by adding the output gap as an explanatory variable and testing to see if it is significant. If the Fed actually looks at the output gap and not the unemployment rate, the output gap should be significant, and the unemployment rate should not be significant when both are included as explanatory variables. In fact, when the output gap was included, it was not significant, and the unemployment rate remained significant. These results thus favor the use of the unemployment rate over the output gap. The same conclusion was reached when the variables for the change in the output gap and the change in the unemployment rate were compared. When both variables were added, the change in the output gap was not significant, and the change in the unemployment rate was.

As discussed in Chapter 2, when deciding between two possible explanatory variables, a common procedure is to run a horse race. If one variable has a t-statistic that is greater than 2.0 or less than −2.0 and the other does not, the first variable wins. In this case, the race was between the unemployment rate and the output gap, and the unemployment rate won.

Examine the Results

We can use our results to see how much the Fed changes the bill rate when inflation changes. Say that inflation increased by 1 percentage point (from, say, 2 percent to 3 percent). How much would the bill rate be predicted to increase? The coefficient for inflation in Box 11-2 is 0.066, so the increase in the first quarter would be 0.066 (from say 2.0 percent to 2.066 percent). This does not seem that large, but we are not finished. Remember that the Fed tends to move slowly, as reflected in the large coefficient of 0.908 for the bill rate lagged. Given that the change in the first quarter was 0.066, the change in the second quarter (from the already higher first quarter value) is 0.908 times 0.066, or .060. The change in the third quarter is 0.908 times 0.060, or 0.054, and so on through as many quarters as we want to consider. If we add all the changes (0.066,

0.060, 0.054, and so on), we get 0.72. Therefore, in the long run, the bill rate changes by 0.72 percentage points when inflation changes by 1.0 percentage point. (Actually, the changes after the initial 0.066 change in the first quarter are not quite 0.060, 0.054, and so on because the change in the bill-rate variables has an effect, but the long-run change is 0.72.)

We can also use our results to see how much the Fed is predicted to change the bill rate when the unemployment rate changes. Suppose the unemployment rate rises by 1 percentage point (from, say, 4 percent to 5 percent). How much would the bill rate be predicted to decrease? The coefficient for the unemployment rate is –0.082, and the coefficient for the change in the unemployment rate is –0.647. The decrease in the bill rate in the first quarter would thus be .082 plus 0.647, or 0.729. The results thus say that if the unemployment rate did rise in one quarter by 1 percentage point, which is a large increase in one quarter, the Fed would aggressively respond by lowering the bill rate in the quarter by 0.729 percentage points. The long-run change in the bill rate is harder to calculate for an unemployment rate change than for an inflation change because the unemployment rate appears in both level and change form, but this can be done. I did the calculation, and the long-run decrease in the bill rate in response to a 1 percentage point increase in the unemployment rate is 0.89 percentage points. The Fed is thus predicted to be fairly aggressive in fighting unemployment.

Given that the Fed is predicted to be aggressive in fighting unemployment, it is interesting to see what it did during the 2008–2009 recession in the United States. As almost everyone knows, a serious recession began in late 2007. The unemployment rate rose rapidly—from 4.8 percent in the fourth quarter of 2007 to 10.0 percent in the fourth quarter of 2009, and inflation remained low. The estimates in this chapter thus suggest that the Fed should have lowered the bill rate substantially. This is exactly what it did. The actual values of the bill rate for 2007:1–2010:2—the actual decisions of the Fed—are presented in Figure 11-3. The bill rate fell from 4.3 percent in 2007:3 to 0.3 percent in 2008:4. In about a year, the Fed lowered the bill rate to essentially zero.

We can use the coefficients in Box 11-2 and the actual values for inflation and the unemployment rate to make predictions of the bill rate. If we knew what inflation and the unemployment rate were for a given quarter, what would be the prediction of the bill rate for that quarter

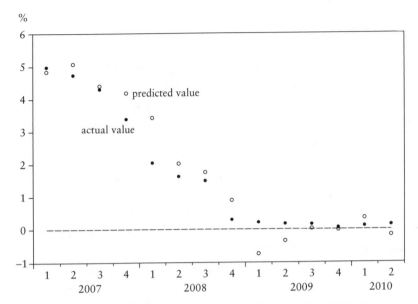

FIGURE **11-3** Actual and predicted values of the bill rate 2007:1–2010:2

using the coefficients in Box 11-2? We have made these predictions for 2007:1–2010:2, and they are also presented in Figure 11-3. You can see that the large decrease in the bill rate is predicted fairly well. The predicted values fall as the actual values fall. The largest error is in 2008:1, where the large fall in the actual value was not predicted. But in general, the prediction errors are fairly small. The Fed aggressively lowered the bill rate to fight unemployment, and it was predicted to do so.

An interesting feature of Figure 11-3 is that three of the predicted values are negative. In 2009:1, the actual value of the bill rate was 0.2 percent, and the predicted value was –0.8 percent. In 2009:2, the actual value was 0.2 percent, and the predicted value was –0.4 percent. In 2010:2, the last quarter of the sample period, the actual value was 0.1 percent, and the predicted value was –0.2 percent. The Fed, of course, cannot drive the bill rate below zero, and what the predicted values are saying is that given the actual values of inflation and the unemployment rate in these three quarters, the Fed would have driven the bill rate below zero if it could have. In 2009 and 2010, the monetary policy of the Fed was constrained by the fact that the bill rate cannot be negative.

Predict Future Fed Behavior

As mentioned above, stock market analysts hang on every word the Fed chairman says, hoping for clues as to what he will do in the future regarding interest rates. But we can make a prediction as to what the chairman will do without having to follow him around looking for clues. The catch, however, is that we need to make predictions about future inflation and the unemployment rate first. Given such predictions, the coefficients in Box 11-2 can be used to make future predictions of the bill rate—future predictions of Fed behavior. The following example shows how this is done.

Assume we are in the last day of the second quarter of 2010 (June 30, 2010). We know (or have good estimates of) the growth of the money supply in the second quarter, the bill rate for the second quarter, the changes in the bill rate for the first and second quarters, and the unemployment rate for the second quarter. We want to predict what the bill rate will be in the third quarter of 2010—in the next three months. We have everything we need to know except the values of inflation and the unemployment rate for the third quarter of 2010. If we make assumptions about these two values, we can predict the bill rate.

Box 11-3 computes the prediction of the bill rate for the third quarter of 2010 using a value of 0.76 percent for inflation and 9.58 percent for the unemployment rate. You can see that the bill rate is predicted to be 0.19 percent. The actual value of the bill rate for the previous quarter (second quarter of 2010) was 0.15 percent, so this prediction is essentially for the bill rate to remain unchanged. The Fed is predicted to continue to keep the bill rate close to zero. We have made this prediction without knowing anything about what the chairman might have been saying at the time. The prediction of a low bill rate is, of course, not surprising. The unemployment rate is high (9.58 percent) and inflation is low (0.76 percent), and the Fed is fighting unemployment.

How accurate is the prediction of 0.19 percent? As shown in the box, the actual value of the bill rate in the third quarter of 2010 was 0.16 percent. The error is thus 0.03 percentage points. This error is small compared to the standard error of 0.47 percentage points, and in this sense, the prediction is quite good. The values that were used for the explanatory variables in Box 11-3, including the values for inflation and

BOX **11-3**

Predicted value of the bill rate for 2010:3			
coef.	value	coef. × value	
0.066	0.76	0.05	inflation
−0.082	9.58	−0.79	unemployment rate
−0.647	−0.11	0.07	change in unemployment rate
0.010	12.11	0.12	money growth lagged
0.223	0.00	0.00	money growth lagged—early Volcker
0.908	0.15	0.14	bill rate lagged
0.279	0.04	0.01	change in bill rate lagged
−0.307	0.05	−0.02	change in bill rate lagged twice
0.61	1.00	0.61	intercept
		0.19	TOTAL (predicted)
		0.16	Actual
		0.03	Error

the unemployment rate, are the actual values, and so the prediction of the bill rate includes no errors from the explanatory variables. This is the type of prediction that is relevant for testing theories, so the small error provides support for the theory. This prediction is not, however, one that could have been made in real time because the actual values for inflation and the unemployment rate would not have been known at the time the prediction was made.

In many cases, we are interested in predictions more than one quarter ahead. In the present example, we might also be interested in the prediction of the bill rate for the fourth quarter of 2010. Given that we have made a prediction for the third quarter of 2010, we can easily make one for the fourth quarter of 2010. We need to make assumptions about the values of inflation and the unemployment rate for the fourth quarter of 2010, and we need to make an assumption about the growth rate of the money supply for the third quarter of 2010. Given these three values, and given what we have predicted the bill rate to be in the third quarter of 2010, we can predict the bill rate for the fourth quarter of

2010. We can then predict the first quarter of 2011 and so on. The prediction of the bill rate for each quarter uses the prediction from the previous quarter, so the predictions build on each other.

Since inflation plays a key role in this story, it would be nice to know how inflation is determined. Can we predict inflation? The answer is yes, and it's on to the next chapter.

12   Inflation

We saw in Chapter 3 that inflation has an effect on voting behavior. If inflation is high at election time, voters tend to vote against the incumbent party, other things being equal. We saw in the last chapter that the Fed raises interest rates when inflation is high to try to bring it down. Inflation has some powerful enemies.

In this chapter, we are concerned with trying to explain how inflation is determined. Why is it sometimes high, as in much of the 1970s, and why is it sometimes low, as in the decades of the 1990s and 2000s. We proceed in the usual way: propose a theory, collect data, use the data to test the theory, think about pitfalls, examine the results, and make a prediction.

We should first be precise about what we mean by inflation. We begin with a measure of the overall price level in the economy. The government computes a number of measures of the overall price level. Some of the more popular ones are (1) the consumer price index, (2) the producer price index, (3) a price index for the total output of the economy (GDP), and (4) a price index for the output of all firms in the economy (this excludes government output). A price index is sometimes called a price level. The percentage change in a price index—that is, how much the price index changes from one period to the next in percentage terms—is called inflation. Inflation is thus the percentage change in some measure of an overall price level. For purposes of this chapter, we will use the fourth price index just listed, namely. the price index for the output of all firms in the economy.

We will present a theory of how firms set prices. We will then use this theory to consider the likely effects on the overall price level. If we explain the overall price level, we also explain inflation, since inflation is just the percentage change in the overall price level.

A Theory of Price Setting Behavior

Let's begin by considering a single firm producing a single good. Some firms have no control over the price of their good. A wheat farmer, for example, has no control over the price of wheat. The farmer can sell as much wheat as he or she wants at the current price. If the farmer would like to charge a higher price for the wheat, tough luck. He or she would sell no wheat. On the other hand, the price does not fall if the farmer sells more wheat.

Many firms have some control over the price they charge for their good, and these are the firms we are interested in. If this type of firm raises its price, it will sell fewer items, but the demand will not fall to zero as it does for the wheat farmer. If the firm wants to sell more items, it must lower its price. We thus have a firm that can change the number of items that it sells by changing its price. We are interested in what influences the firm's choice of its price.

A common assumption in economics is that firms maximize profits; they make choices that lead to their profits being as high as possible given the constraints they face. We will make this assumption in this chapter. We will assume that a firm sets its price to maximize its profits. If profits can be increased by raising the price, the firm will do so; conversely, if profits can be increased by lowering the price, the firm will do so.

Let's consider a firm that is producing 50 items and selling them at a price of $10 per item. The firm's revenue is thus $500. Say that it costs $300 to produce the 50 items. The firm's profit is thus $200. Is this the best that the firm can do? To answer this, we need to consider what happens if the firm raises or lowers its output by 1 item. If the firm produces 51 items, it must lower the price a little to sell 51 instead of 50. Say that it needs to lower the price to $9.95 per item. Its revenue is then 51 times $9.95, or $507.45. The increase in revenue is thus $7.45. Note that the increase in revenue from selling the extra item is less than the price of the item because the firm has to lower its price to all customers. (We assume that the firm has to charge the same price to everyone.)

Next we must consider what it costs the firm to produce the extra item. We know that it costs $300 to produce 50 items, which is an average of $6 per item. A common assumption in economics is that the cost of producing an additional item rises as the number of items produced rises. If moving from 40 to 41 items costs an additional $5, moving from 41 to 42 items might cost an additional $5.05. Firms are assumed to run into capacity problems as production rises, which are costly. A firm may, for example, have to pay more for overtime work, or it may have to use older machines that cost more to run per hour. So even though the average cost of the 50 items is $6 per item, the cost of producing the 51st item may be more. If the additional cost is $8, it would not pay the firm to produce the extra item because it would receive only $7.45 in additional revenue.

What if the firm produced 49 instead of 50 items? In this case, it can raise its price because it is selling one less item. Say that it could raise its price to $10.05. Its revenue is then 49 times $10.05, or $492.45. The decrease in revenue is thus $7.55. Note that the decrease in revenue from selling one less item is not as large as the price of the item because the firm charges the higher price to all customers.

What about cost when the firm lowers production? If the cost per item rises as production rises, then the cost *saving* obviously falls when production falls. If moving from 50 to 51 items costs an additional $8, it may be that moving from 50 to 49 items saves an amount less than $8. Let's assume the cost saving is $7.50. In this case, it would not pay the firm to cut production because revenue would fall by $7.55 and cost falls by only $7.50.

Given these numbers, our firm is maximizing its profits by producing 50 items. Profits fall if it either raises or lowers production. In general, a firm keeps raising its production (and thus lowering its price) until the extra revenue it receives is less than the extra cost it incurs.

So what? Well, we are now ready to see what changes a firm's pricing behavior. Say there is an increase in the demand for a firm's good. How will the firm respond? If the firm kept its price at $10, it could sell more items, maybe 60. However, producing the extra 10 items would be costly if the cost per item rises as production rises. It will likely pay the firm to produce fewer than 60 and raise its price. The profit maximizing point might be, for example, where production is 55 items and the price is $11 per item. Again, the firm would move to the point where any change in production would lead to a fall in profits.

If demand for the firm's good fell, the opposite would happen. If demand fell and the firm kept its price at $10, it would sell fewer items, maybe 40. However, the cost per additional item is lower when production is lower, and it will likely pay the firm to produce more than 40 and lower its price. The new profit maximizing point might be, for example, where production is 45 items and the price is $9 per item.

We have thus seen that an increase in demand leads the firm to raise its price, and a decrease in demand leads the firm to lower its price. This is the first main point of the theory.

The second main point concern costs. Say that the firm uses oil in producing its good and that the price of oil rises. Assume that demand for the firm's good remains unchanged so that the firm could still sell 50 items at a price of $10 per item. After the oil price increase, however, 50 units may no longer be the profit maximizing point. Moving from 50 to 49 units now saves more in costs because the cost saving on oil is greater (because of the higher price of oil). Now perhaps the cost saving in moving from 50 to 49 is $9.50 rather than $7.50. The firm is thus likely to benefit from lowering its production and raising its price. The new profit maximizing point might be where production is 45 units and the price is $11 per unit.

The opposite happens when the price of oil falls: the firm would increase production and lower its price. Thus, the second main point is that costs have a positive effect on price: when costs rise, the price rises and vice versa.

The last main issue to consider is the speed with which firms respond to changes in demand and costs. We saw in the last chapter that the Fed tends to respond slowly to changes. We captured this idea by using the previous period's bill rate as an explanatory variable. Firms also appear to respond slowly, and we will capture this by using the previous period's price as an explanatory variable.

We now move from a single firm to the whole economy. Using the theory of the price setting behavior of a firm, we will assume that the price level in the economy depends on some measure of demand in the economy and some measure of costs. We will use as the measure of demand the unemployment rate. When the unemployment rate is low, the economy is booming and demand is high. When the unemployment rate is high, the economy is in recession and demand is low. We thus expect from the theory that the unemployment rate should have a negative effect on the price level: a decrease in the unemployment rate should lead to a rise in the price level and vice versa.

We will use two variables to measure costs. The first is a measure of the overall price of imports, which we will call the *cost of imports*. This is a price index of all goods that are imported. Many firms use imports in their production processes, and when the cost of imports rises, firms' costs rise. For example, one of the key goods that is imported is oil, and oil is a cost to many firms. The other measure of costs is the average wage rate in the economy, which we will call the *wage rate*. Wages are a key cost to almost all firms, so when wage rates rise, costs rise. We expect from the theory that the cost of imports and the wage rate should have a positive effect on the price level.

We also expect the lagged price level to have an effect on the current price level because firms take time to adjust to new situations.

We need to consider one other issue before summarizing the theory. For the time period we consider, which is from 1954 to the present, the price level has an upward trend. Other things being equal, the price level tends to increase each period. This is not something that the above theory explains, and so to account for this, a *trend* variable is added. This is a variable that simply increases by 1 each quarter.

The theory is summarized in Box 12-1.

BOX **12-1**

price level depends on:	
	unemployment rate
	wage rate
	cost of imports
	price level lagged
	trend
	intercept

The Data

As was the case for the theory of Fed behavior in the last chapter, the data that we need to test the theory of price setting behavior are easy to come by. The government compiles data on the price level, the unemployment rate, the wage rate, and the cost of imports (the import price level). Remember that the price level is the price index for the output of all firms in the economy. We will use quarterly data, and the period we will consider is the first quarter of 1954 through the second quarter of 2010. There are 226 quarters within this period, so we have 226 observations.

In many cases in economics, including the present one, we need to consider whether the variables should be used in their natural units or in percentage terms. For variables like the price level, the cost of imports, and the wage rate, it is usually more appropriate to have them in percentage terms. If a firm's initial price is $5 and it decides on a new price of $6, this is a much larger percentage increase than if the initial price is $10 and the new price is $11. It is likely that the firm is thinking more in percentage terms than in absolute terms. We will thus use the price level, the cost of imports, and the wage rate in percentage terms. (This means using the logarithm of each variable, although it is not really necessary to know this. Just think that the three variables are in percentage terms.)

The data on the price level and the cost of imports are plotted in Figure 12-1. The figure shows that there was almost no increase in the cost of imports in the 1950s and 1960s. There were huge increases in the 1970s, due in large part to huge increases in the price of oil. The cost of imports fell slightly in the first half of the 1980s, rose slightly in the last half of the 1980s, and did not change much in the 1990s and 2000s.

The most rapid increase in the price level occurred in the 1970s, which is also the period of the huge increases in the cost of imports. It thus seems likely that the cost of imports has a positive effect on the price level, which is consistent with the theory that costs affect the price setting behavior of firms.

Fit and Test

As always, we use a computer to find the set of coefficients that leads to the smallest sum of squared errors. In this case, there are 226

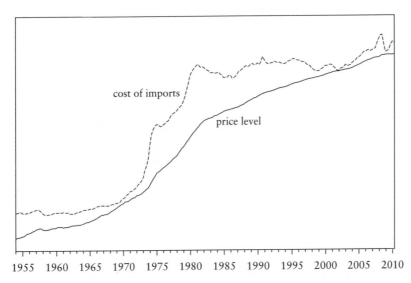

FIGURE **12-1**   Price level and cost of imports 1954:1–2010:2

errors for each set of coefficients tried. We have a similar problem here of causality in both directions that we had in the last chapter: the price level affects the unemployment rate and the wage rate, and the unemployment rate and the wage rate affect the price level. We have to purge the effects of the price level on the unemployment rate and the wage rate before we use them as explanatory variables. We use the same method here as we used in the last chapter. The best fit is the one that leads to the smallest sum of squared errors using the purged variables as explanatory variables.

The results are shown in Box 12-2. The coefficient for the unemployment rate is –0.182 with a t-statistic of –8.74. The unemployment rate is thus significant, and it has a negative effect on the price level: a decrease in the unemployment rate leads to an increase in the price level. The coefficients for the two cost variables, the wage rate and the cost of imports, are 0.033 and 0.050 with t-statistics of 2.96 and 21.52. These variables are also significant, and both have a positive effect on the price level. The significance of the cost of imports is, of course, not surprising given what we know from Figure 12-1.

BOX **12-2**

price level depends on:		t-statistic
−0.182	unemployment rate	−8.74
0.033	wage rate	2.96
0.050	cost of imports	21.52
0.891	price level lagged	95.96
0.029	trend	9.17
−3.69	intercept	−3.44
standard error: 0.37		
number of observations: 226		

The coefficient for the price level lagged is 0.891 with a t-statistic of 95.96, which is strong evidence that a firm's price last period has an important effect on the price that it chooses this period.

The trend variable has a positive coefficient, as expected, and it is significant. This shows that regardless of the other variables, the price level has a positive trend. In other words, there is a tendency for the price level to rise over time independent of anything else.

The standard error is 0.37 percentage points, which is fairly small. It says that 68.2 percent of the time the error in predicting the price level should be between −0.37 and 0.37 percentage points.

Remember that inflation is just the percentage change in the price level, so if we know what affects the price level, we know what affects inflation. We can thus say that the main causes of inflation are demand, as measured by the unemployment rate, and costs, as measured by the cost of imports and the wage rate.

Possible Pitfalls

The results in Box 12-2 have one unreasonable implication, which concerns the size of the effect of a change in the unemployment rate on the price level. The coefficient for the unemployment rate tells us that a decrease in the unemployment rate of, say, 1 percentage point leads to an increase in the price level of 0.182 percentage points in first quarter. This 0.182 value is the same regardless of the initial size of the unemployment rate. It does not matter whether the fall of 1 percentage point was from an unemployment rate of 10 percent or 4 percent. It is not reasonable, however, to assume that the 0.182 value holds for very low values of the unemployment rate.

This point can be seen in Figure 12-2. Case 1 pertains to the present results. Other things being equal, the relationship between the price

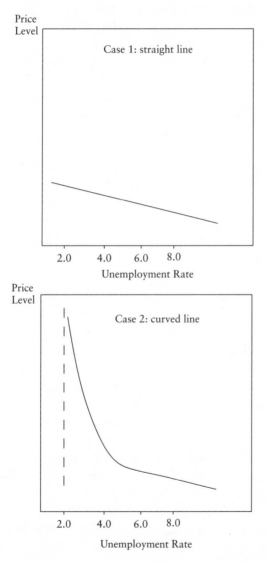

FIGURE **12-2**   Relationship between the price level and the unemployment rate (other things being equal)

level and the unemployment rate is represented by a straight line. The slope of the line is constant. Case 2 depicts a situation that seems more reasonable. It says that as the unemployment rate gets closer and closer to a small number, which is assumed to be 2.0 percent in the figure, the price level rises at an increasing rate. In this case, lowering the unemployment rate by 1 percentage point has a much larger effect on the price level when the unemployment rate is close to 2.0 than when it is not.

You might ask, why did we use case 1 when case 2 seems more reasonable? The answer is that we don't have enough observations on the curved part of the line in case 2 to determine where the bend in the line starts and how steep it becomes. Most of our observations are for unemployment rates above 4.0 percent. If the line to the right of 4.0 is roughly straight, as drawn in case 2, then all we can do with our observations is determine the slope of the straight line.

This means that we cannot use our results to predict with any confidence what would happen to the price level if the unemployment rate fell much below 4.0 percent. We simply have no historical experience to guide us. This is an important pitfall but one we can do nothing about, except limit any use of the coefficients to situations in which the unemployment rate is not extremely low. We will come back to this problem at the end of this chapter.

Another possible pitfall is the use of the unemployment rate as the measure of demand in the economy. There are many possible measures, and the unemployment rate may not be the best one. An alternative measure is the output gap, which was discussed in the last chapter. Remember that the output gap is the difference between potential output and actual output. We can test the output gap versus the unemployment rate by adding the output gap as an explanatory variable and seeing if it is significant. If the price level responds more to the output gap than to the unemployment rate, the output gap should be significant but not the unemployment rate. This is the standard horse race test discussed in Chapter 2. When the output gap was added, it was not significant, and the unemployment rate remained significant. These results thus favor the use of the unemployment rate over the output gap. This is the same conclusion that was reached in the last chapter regarding the explanation of the bill rate.

Another possible pitfall concerns the use of the price level lagged as an explanatory variable. Does this adequately capture the price adjustment behavior of firms? Perhaps the price level lagged twice should also be an explanatory variable. This was tested by adding the price level lagged twice, and it was not significant. There is thus no evidence on this score that the adjustment process is inadequately captured.

There are many views in economics about the best way to explain inflation, and the present results would not be accepted by everyone as being any good. The idea that demand and costs affect inflation is accepted by nearly everyone. Some of the disagreements are about how to measure demand, but the more important disagreements concern price adjustment issues. Some would argue that the dependent variable should be inflation, not the price level, and some would argue that the dependent variable should be the *change* in inflation. If either of these views is right, the price level lagged twice should be significant when added to the present results. It is not, so this is at least some evidence against these views. This debate is, however, far from over.

Examine the Results and Predict

As discussed in the previous section, we should not use the results to examine situations in which the unemployment rate is much below 4.0 percent. You should thus take the following discussion as pertaining only to situations where the unemployment rate remains above about 4.0 percent.

The coefficient for the unemployment rate is −0.182, which says that the price level rises 0.182 percent in the first quarter after a fall in the unemployment rate of 1 percentage point. Because of the effect of the lagged price level, in the next quarter the price level rises .891 times 0.182, or 0.162 percent. In the quarter after that, it rises .891 times 0.162, or 0.144 percent, and so on. We can add all these changes up, and if we do so, we get a total for the long-run increase in the price level of 1.67 percent. This is, however, a little misleading, since when the price level rises, the wage rate is likely to rise, and we have not taken this into account. If we did take the wage rate into account (which would require results explaining the wage rate), the long-run response would be higher. An increase in the price level leads to an increase in the wage rate, which in turn leads to a further increase in the price level, and so on. We can thus say here that the long-run response of the price level to a fall in the unemployment rate of 1.0 percentage point is *at least* 1.67 percent.

The coefficient for the cost of imports is 0.050, so an increase in the cost of imports of 10 percent would lead to an increase in the price level of 0.50 percent in the initial quarter. In the next quarter, the increase would be 0.891 times 0.50, or 0.45, and so on. The long-run response is 4.59 percent. This is a fairly large response. It says that in the long run, the price level rises by close to a half of any increase in the cost of imports. Again, Figure 12-1 shows why this effect is estimated to be so large. Large changes in the cost of imports are bad news for policy makers because they have such large effects on the price level.

The coefficient for the wage rate is 0.033, and so an increase in the wage rate of 10 percent would lead to an increase in the price level of 0.33 percent in the initial quarter. In the next quarter, the increase would be 0.891 times 0.033, or 0.029, and so on. The long-run response is 3.03 percent. Again, this is an underestimate because the price level affects the wage rate as well as vice versa. To be more precise, we would need to explain the wage rate and then use these results along with the price level results to examine long-run effects.

Just as we predicted the bill rate in the last chapter, we can predict inflation in this chapter. For example, if we are at the beginning of the third quarter of 2010, we know or have a good estimate of the price level for the second quarter of 2010. If we want to predict what the price level will be in the third quarter of 2010, we need to make assumptions about the unemployment rate, the wage rate, and the cost of imports for the third quarter of 2010. If we make assumptions about these three values, we can use the coefficients in Box 12-2 to predict the price level for the third quarter of 2010. The predicted inflation rate is then simply the predicted percentage change in the price level. We can then go on and make a prediction for the fourth quarter of 2010 and so on.

I will not present any calculations here. The procedure is the same as in the last chapter for the calculations of the bill-rate predictions.

Inflation and the Fed

We know from the last chapter that the Fed raises the interest rate when inflation increases. We know from this chapter that inflation increases when the unemployment rate decreases, the cost of imports increases, and the wage rate increases. The Fed also knows this, and it watches closely for signs that labor markets are getting tight, that import costs like oil prices are rising, or that wage rates are rising. At the beginning of 2000, the unemployment rate was low and oil prices had risen substantially. The Fed was thus concerned that inflation was going to increase, and it raised the interest rate three times between February and May 2000. The total increase was 1.0 percentage point.

A risk that the Fed faced in 2000 was the possibility that case 2 in Figure 12-2 was true and that the economy was near the point where the line starts to get steep. As long as the economy is on the straight line in the figure, the cost of not tightening enough in terms of an increase in the price level is fairly modest. On the other hand, if the economy is near the bend and the unemployment rate falls into this zone, the increase in the price level could be quite large.

Alas, this is where the tools that have been discussed in this book are of little help. As discussed above, we have too few observations at very low unemployment rates to be able to determine where the bend occurs. In this sense, the Fed was groping in the dark in 2000, having little historical experience to guide it. From the point of view of a social scientist, it would have been useful if the economy had moved into the bad inflation zone. This would have finally allowed estimates to be made of where the bend begins and how fast the line curves up—not that we should hope this ever happens. This would be a high price for society to pay for better estimates.

The economy did not in fact go into a bad inflation zone in 2000, and by 2001, a significant slowdown had begun. The Fed switched from worrying about inflation to worrying about unemployment. At the time of this writing (November 2010), unemployment remains high and inflation remains low. Although inflation has not been a problem for many years, if it ever comes back, Box 12-2 says that the Fed will fight it.

13 More Things

The aim of this book has been to give the nontechnical reader a sense of how social scientists use statistical tools to try to explain behavior. The steps of proposing a theory, collecting data, fitting the data, using the data to test the theory, thinking about pitfalls, examining the results, and making predictions have been used in each chapter. If the tests do not support the theory or if the pitfalls seem serious, the last two steps are not of much interest. We must have some confidence in the results before using them.

One of the main limitations in the social sciences is the absence of good data to test theories. We saw this in the chapter on extramarital affairs, where the two surveys that were used were far from ideal. When thinking about pitfalls, the first question to consider is how good the data are.

This book has only scratched the surface regarding empirical work in the social sciences. A useful type of data that has not been considered is one in which observations are available on many individuals over many time periods. The same people, for example, may have been surveyed once a year for many years. With this type of data, it is possible to examine how behavior changes across people as well as across time. The same methodology of theory, data, fitting, testing, and so forth can be used.

A similar type of data is where there are observations across states or cities as well as across time. In examining voting behavior, for example, we can get data on votes for president by state. Data are also available across countries as well as across time. For example, observations on interest rates, unemployment rates, and inflation are available for most countries in the world over many years.

Many theories, especially in economics, concern more than one dependent variable at the same time. We briefly mentioned this in the last two chapters. The bill rate affects inflation and the unemployment rate as well as vice versa, and the price level affects the unemployment rate and the wage rate as well as vice versa. As noted in the two chapters, there are statistical methods for dealing with such cases. These methods are part of the best fitting type of methods, so the insights from Chapter 2 are still relevant. The general idea is to find a set of coefficients that fits the data well. Tests are available that are similar to tests using t-statistics. The general testing procedure is to compute the probability that we would get the particular answer we did if our theory is wrong. If the computed probability is low (like a large t-statistic), then the data support the theory, aside from possible pitfall problems.

W. H. Auden aside, I hope this book has given you a deeper appreciation of what social scientists do.

Chapter Notes

Chapter 1

The material in this chapter and in Chapter 3 is taken from a series of papers I did on votes for president. The first one is Ray C. Fair, "The Effect of Economic Events on Votes for President," *The Review of Economics and Statistics* (1978): 159–173; the least technical discussion is in Ray C. Fair, "Econometrics and Presidential Elections," *Journal of Economic Perspectives* (1996): 89–102; and the latest two are Ray C. Fair, "Presidential and Congressional Vote-Share Equations," *American Journal of Political Science* (2009): 55–72, and "Presidential and Congressional Vote-Share Equations: November 2010 Update," unpublished (November 11, 2010).

A study that showed that people remember peak stimuli more than average stimuli is Donald A. Redelmeier and Daniel Kahneman, "Patients' Memories of Painful Medical Treatments: Real-Time and Retrospective Evaluations of Two Minimally Invasive Procedures," *Pain* (1996): 3–8. This study showed that people also tend to remember the last part of the experiment more than otherwise, which is consistent with the use of the growth rate in the year of the election as one of the variables explaining voting behavior.

Chapter 2

I have tried to present the material in this chapter in an intuitive way without saying anything wrong—under the assumption that the errors are normally distributed. To be exact, Figure 2-4 should be a *t*-distribution and not a normal distribution, and I have stated in the text that the normal distribution in the figure is only an approximation.

Chapter 3

The results in this chapter are taken from the paper listed under Chapter 1 dated November 11, 2010. The coefficients in Box 3-2 remain the same through the 2012 election, but the economic values change as new data become available. The presidential vote prediction is updated on my Web site as new economic data come in. There is also a calculator that allows a user to enter his or her own economic values to obtain a presidential vote prediction.

Chapter 4

This chapter is based on material in the third and fourth references under Chapter 1. Regarding the on-term House election in 2012, the coefficients in Box 4-3 remain the same through the election, but the economic values change as new data become available. Similar to the presidential vote prediction, the House vote prediction is updated on my Web site as new economic data come in. There is also a calculator that allows a user to enter his or her own economic values to obtain a House vote prediction.

Chapter 5

The material in this chapter is taken from Ray C. Fair, "A Theory of Extramarital Affairs," *Journal of Political Economy* (1978): 45–61. I have stated in the chapter that something that increases the utility from the affair has a positive effect on time spent in the affair. This seems likely, but the effect in the theoretical model is not unambiguous—see pages 50–51 of the paper. The unambiguity comes from a subtle income effect. The estimator used is the Tobit estimator—James Tobin, "Estimation of Relationships for Limited Dependent Variables," *Econometrica* (1958): 24–36.

John F. Macdonald and Robert A. Moffitt, "The Uses of Tobit Analysis," *The Review of Economics and Statistics* (May 1980): 318–321, point out that Tobit coefficient estimates do not accurately measure the change in the expected dependent variable (affairs in this chapter) except for observations far above the zero limit. The numbers used in this book's discussion are thus only approximate.

Chapter 6

As noted in the text, this chapter is taken from an article by Orley Ashenfelter, David Ashmore, and Robert Lalonde, "Bordeaux Wine Vintage Quality and the Weather," *Chance* (1995): 7–14. The authors supplied me with the data, and I duplicated their results. The wine merchant I used was Mt. Carmel Wine, North Haven, Connecticut.

Chapter 7

As noted in the text, this chapter is taken from an article by Garey C. Durden and Larry V. Ellis, "The Effects of Attendance on Student Learning in Principles of Economics," *American Economic Review* (May 1995): 343–346. Box 7-1 is taken from their Table 2.

Chapter 8

The material in this chapter is taken from Ray C. Fair, "How Fast Do Old Men Slow Down?" *The Review of Economics and Statistics* (1994): 103–118, and "Estimated Age Effects in Athletic Events and Chess," *Experimental Aging Research* (2007): 37–57. The estimation method used is a combination of the polynomial-spline method and the frontier-function method.

As noted in the text, my Web site allows a user to enter his or her time at an event and age at the time the event took place and receive back potential times by age.

Chapter 9

The material in this chapter is taken from Ray C. Fair, "'Estimated Age Effects in Baseball," *Journal of Quantitative Analysis in Sports* (2008): http://www.bepress.com/jqas/vol4/iss1/1/. The "height" values in Tables 9-2, 9-3, and 9-4 differ from the values in the equivalent tables in this paper. In each table in the paper, the values labeled "CNST" have a constant added to them in Tables 9-2, 9-3, and 9-4 to convert them to the height of the curve in Figure 9-1 at the peak age. The constants are, respectively, 0.387, 0.120, and –2.023.

Chapter 10

The material in this chapter is taken from Ray C. Fair and John F. Oster, "College Football Rankings and Market Efficiency," *Journal of Sports Economics* (2007): 3–18. Some of the data were sent via e-mail by Mr. Massey.

Chapter 11

The first example of an estimated interest rate rule is in William G. Dewald and Harry G. Johnson, "An Objective Analysis of the Objectives of American Monetary Policy, 1952–61," in Deane Carson, ed., *Banking and Monetary Studies*, (Homewood, Ill.: Richard D. Irwin, 1963): 171–189. I first used an estimated rule in my U.S. macroeconometric model in Ray C. Fair, "The Sensitivity of Fiscal Policy Effects to Assumptions About the Behavior of the Federal Reserve," *Econometrica* (1978): 1165–1179. These rules are sometimes referred to as "Taylor rules," named after Professor John Taylor at Stanford. Taylor discusses interest rate rules in John B. Taylor, "Discretion Versus Policy Rules in Practice," *Carnegie-Rochester Series on Public Policy*, 39 (1993): 195–214. These rules should probably be called Dewald-Johnson rules, since Dewald and Johnson preceded Taylor by about 30 years.

The specification in Box 11-2 is equation 30 in Ray C. Fair, *Estimating How the Macroeconomy Works* (Cambridge, Mass.: Harvard University Press, 2004). The estimates in the box are those dated July 30, 2010, on my Web site. The economic values used in Box 11-3 are those dated October 29, 2010, on my Web site. The estimation method used is two-stage least squares.

Chapter 12

The specification in Box 12-2 is equation 10 in Ray C. Fair, *Estimating How the Macroeconomy Works* (Cambridge, Mass.: Harvard University Press, 2004). The estimates in the box are those dated July 30, 2010, on my Web site. The estimation method used is two-stage least squares.

Glossary

- **coefficient**—A number, like the value of a slope. A set of coefficients is determined by finding the set that leads to the smallest sum of squared errors.
- **data mining**—Trying many explanatory variables and choosing those that lead to the best fit. Doing this increases the chances that the results are a fluke.
- **dependent variable**—The variable explained by the theory.
- **explanatory variable**—The variables that the theory says affect the dependent variable.
- **highly significant**—Coefficients with large t-statistics in absolute value.
- **horse race**—Including two or more competing explanatory variables in the analysis and seeing if one is significant and the others are not.
- **income effect**—The effect of a change in nonwage income on behavior. An increase in nonwage income leads people to work less and consume more and vice versa for a decrease.
- **independent variable**—Same as explanatory variable.
- **omitted variable bias**—The estimated coefficient for an explanatory variable is biased because some other explanatory variable has been omitted that truly affects the dependent variable and that is also related to the particular explanatory variable.
- **other things being equal**—Holding everything else the same. Nothing changes except the one thing being considered at the time.
- **precise estimates**—Same as highly significant.

- **real-time prediction**—A prediction made before the value of the dependent variable is known.
- **selection bias**—Occurs when the probability that a person answers a survey depends on the size of the dependent variable, that is, the variable the theory is trying to explain.
- **significant**—A coefficient value is significant if the probability is small that we would get that value if the true coefficient were zero. We are using a cut-off probability of about 5 percent in this book, which is conventional.
- **standard error of the estimated slope**—A measure of the size of a typical error that is made when determining a slope.
- **standard error of the line**—A measure of the size of a typical error.
- *t***-statistic**—The ratio of a coefficient value to its standard error (the standard error of the estimated slope for that coefficient). A t-statistic greater than 2.0 or less than –2.0 means it is very unlikely that the true value of the coefficient is zero.
- **variable**—Something that changes, for instance, across time or across people.

Poetry Credits

Introduction

W. H. Auden, *Under Which Lyre*

"Under Which Lyre: A Reactionary Tract for the Times," copyright © 1976 by Edward Mendelson, William Meredith, and Monroe K. Spears, Executors of the Estate of W. H. Auden, from COLLECTED POEMS OF W. H. AUDEN by W. H. Auden. Used by permission of Random House, Inc.

Chapter 2

J. V. Cunningham, *Meditation on Statistical Method*

From *The Poems of J. V. Cunningham, edited with an Introduction and Commentary by Timothy Steele*. Reprinted by permission of Swallow Press/Ohio University Press, Athens, Ohio (www.ohioswallow.com).

Chapter 3

William Butler Yeats, *Politics*

Reprinted with the permission of Scribner, a Division of Simon & Schuster, Inc., from The COLLECTED WORKS OF W. B. YEATS, VOLUME I: The POEMS, REVISED by W. B. Yeats. Copyright © 1940 by Georgie Yeats, renewed 1968 by Bertha Georgie Yeats, Michael Butler Yeats, and Anne Yeats. All rights reserved.

Index

Transition age, 124–125, 129–132, 134, 137
Trend variable, 193
Truman, H., 6
t-statistics: for college grades and class attendance prediction, 118–120; for congressional election prediction, 72–74; description and definition of, 25, 31–44, 210; for interest rate prediction, 178–179; for marathon times prediction, 130; for presidential election prediction, 52–55; for wine quality prediction, 105–107
Two-party vote, 16

Uncertainty, degree of, 67
Unemployment rate, 176–177, 182–183, 196–200
Utility *vs.* disutility, 86

Variables, 12; addition of, 39–42; dependent, 13, 209; description and definition of, 210; explanatory, 13, 209; horse races of, 209; independent, 13, 209; omitted variable bias, 209; testing for other, 42–43
Vintage, 101
Vintage price, 103–104
Volcker, P., 174–178
Vote share, 9–17, 47–48
Voter knowledge, 62

Voting behavior prediction. *See* Congressional election prediction; Presidential election prediction
Voting behavior theories, 6–13, 46–47, 69–72

Wage rate, 193
Wage *vs.* nonwage income, 86–87
Walker, L., 155, 157
War variable, 49, 69
Weather variables, 103, 105–110, 114
Whittier, J. G., 68
Williams, T., 147–151, 154
Wilson, W., 16
Wine quality prediction: 1855 classification and, 102; actual *vs.* predicted vintage prices, 106; auction market and, 103, 114; data fit for, 105–107; data sets for, 105–107; description and definition of, 101; percentage errors for, 106–107; pitfalls of, 107–109; prediction sets for, 109–114; premiers crus and, 102; result examination of, 114; seconds crus and, 102, 112–114; theories for, 101–105; *t*-statistics for, 105–107; vintage and, 101; vintage price and, 103–104; weather and, 103–105

Yeats, W. B., 46